THE
THEORY
OF
21

CHUCK REAVES

THE
THEORY
OF
21

FINDING THE POWER
TO SUCCEED

M. Evans and Company, Inc.
New York

Library of Congress Cataloging in Publication Data

Reaves, Chuck.
The theory of 21.

1. Success.   2. Psychology, Industrial.   I. Title.
II. Title: Theory of twenty-one.
HF5386.R27 1983   650.1   83-14119

ISBN 0-87131-421-5

M. Evans and Company, Inc.
216 East 49 Street
New York, New York 10017
Design by Lauren Dong
Manufactured in the United States of America
9 8 7 6 5 4 3 2 1

To the three most valuable Twenty-Ones I have known:
Candace
The Preacher
and the One who makes it all possible.

Acknowledgments

I would like to acknowledge several individuals whose example led me to formulate and use The Theory of 21 and then to make this book a reality. Blaine Thacker taught me the value of always playing to win. Bob Ranalli showed me the value of having a plan. Arch McGill demonstrated the heights to which a 21 can rise, and Mark Davies and Rick Harker stretched me beyond my perceived limitations. I am forever in the debt of these men, 21s all.

On a personal level, the 21s who have been my inspiration include Dr. Sam Coker, Wayne Dyer, Paul Dixon and Wally Amos.

My wife Candace deserves much of the credit for this book. Her consistent inspiration in my personal life and professional life was and is invaluable.

Finally, I would like to acknowledge the Twenties who taught me so much about the Theory. They are too numerous and too undeserving to mention individually.

Contents

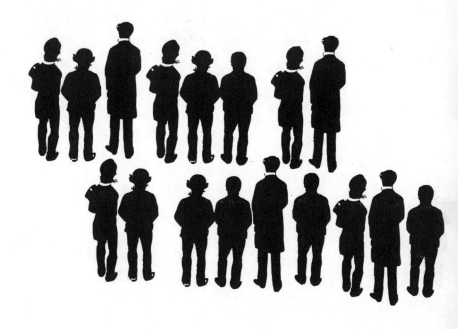

For every person
who will say yes,
there are twenty
who will say no.
For a positive response you must
find the twenty-first person.

THE
THEORY
OF
21

1

THE
QUEST FOR A YES

THE Theory of 21 applies in business—in marketing, in engineering, in manufacturing. The Theory also applies in education, to teachers and students. It applies in churches, civic groups, social organizations, and sororities and fraternities. In fact, the Theory applies to any universe of twenty-one people or more. The reason is: the Theory is part of human nature.

I didn't invent the Theory of 21—I merely recognized it for what it was. Like Sir Isaac Newton, who is said to have made his contribution to science as the result of observing the natural phenomenon of the falling of an apple, I don't necessarily like or dislike the Theory. I may not completely understand the "why" behind the Theory, but only attempt to explain the "what" of the Theory. The Theory has been in effect for a long time—at least since biblical days. There are records of 21 since the advent of written history. Just as gravity was in effect before we named it and began to study it, the Theory of 21 has been in force, and now we can begin to study, understand, and use it.

We may not understand exactly why objects fall perpendicularly to the earth's surface—it certainly would be more interesting if they fell at forty-five-degree angles. We would probably all be better off if objects fell more slowly than they do. But God made gravity as it is, and that's that. All we can do is study it, learn all we can about it, and then find a way to use it to our advantage.

The same is true of the Theory of 21.

We need to learn to use it to our advantage at work, at home, and anytime there is something to be accomplished. That's what this book is all about. After reading this book and observing people in a manner that may be unfamiliar to you now, you will learn to discern which people can really help you and which will actually try to stop or delay you. Then you will be using the Theory of 21 to be more successful at almost anything you attempt.

Sir Isaac Newton

Now, gravity started out as a theory and, after a convincing sales campaign, became the LAW of gravity. It is accepted in all socioeconomic strata all over the world. Every major world power, Third World power, and developing nation and many underdeveloped countries now subscribe to the law of gravity. I am enough of a 21 to believe that the Theory of 21 should receive the same notoriety.

Acceptance of the theory of gravity caused dramatic changes to take place. Babies experimenting with gravity gave rise to unbreakable baby bottles. Young children testing the effects of gravity caused the creation of the training wheel industry. Teenagers challenging the effects of gravity as a form of recreation have caused a surge in the sales of roller skates, elbow pads, knee pads, Ace bandages, and plaster of Paris.

As the Theory of 21 becomes accepted, we can expect dramatic changes in our lives and in the world.

The Theory is based on my observations of a seemingly illogical behavior pattern, one demonstrated over and over by a majority of people. I have seen this behavior in all races, both sexes, all strata of management, and every social and economic class. This behavior is intended to accomplish nothing. It may require a great deal of time and effort, but its goal is to ensure that nothing gets done. You will see, in this book and all around you, evidence of this theory in action. You will observe enormous amounts of resources being expended, in seemingly worthwhile causes, that result in nothing. And they are successes because the goal set was the goal achieved—nothing.

You may be asking yourself, "Why is this happening?" When you have finished this book, you will understand.

The pattern is always the same (although it may be masked, as we will discuss later). For every undertaking there will be twenty people who will find some reason why it cannot be done. They will identify something that is merely an obstacle, declare it to be immovable, stand by it, and defend it rigidly. The obstacle is to be the dead end. I call these people "Twenties."

Twenties have the ability to take even the smallest or flimsiest obstacle and turn it into an absolute dead end. There is little that anyone can do to move Twenties away from their obstacles. Sometimes this ability results from Twentyism, which is a belief—almost a religion—that these people follow zealously. Other times it shows up in the form of Twentyitis, which is an infectious disease that permeates the population. It is easily contracted by the less ambitious and is difficult to cure. It can be spread by those afflicted with Twentyitis, Twentyism, or apathy. In all cases, it flourishes on obstacles.

Obstacles come in three flavors: can't be, shouldn't be, and won't be.

Some of the more frequent "can't be's" are:

> **It can't be done because** . . .
> we've never done it that way before.
> it won't work, don't ask me why.
> it costs too much.
> it violates Rule 97360A7, Section IV A.1.
> it just can't.

Some popular "shouldn't be's" are:

> **It shouldn't be done because** . . .
> it would set a precedent.
> everybody would want one.
> it wouldn't be in the best interests of the customer.
> it just shouldn't.

And finally:

> **It won't be done because** . . .
> so-and-so won't approve it.
> such-and-such department won't allow it.
> nobody will push it.
> it just won't.

Until now, very few people have tried to find or be the

twenty-first person. But that is changing. A growing number of people in all walks of life are accepting the challenge to accomplish the difficult in order to achieve the impossible. Many of these people were stimulated by the successes of other 21s. Others were motivated by the desire to survive, to overcome the threats of competition, economic perils, and other dangers. Whatever the stimulation, 21s have one thing in common: they *achieve*.

America was founded by groups of 21s. Beginning with Columbus, whose Twenties included heads of state and noted scientists, this underdeveloped country came to be a world power because enough people understood and withstood the Theory of 21.

Once you understand the *impact* of being a 21, you'll grasp the *importance* of being a 21. Become a 21 and YOU WILL MAKE A DIFFERENCE!

That's also what this book is about: becoming a 21 and making an impact on your family, your church, your business, your country, and even the world.

Sound like a lot of hype? When you finish this book you will not only be able to recognize the Twenties and the 21s in every situation, but you will also be able to see the impact that the 21s are having. And best of all, you will learn how you, with your current capabilities, can be a 21.

Why should you believe that?

Let's look at some examples, starting with good old Christopher Columbus. You remember the story from grammar school: everybody except Columbus and a few other misfits believed that the world was flat and that if you sailed far enough toward the west you'd fall off. (Remember, it was Columbus *and a few others*; we'll come back to that later.) Columbus believed that if he sailed far enough toward the west he'd wind up east of where he started. That was pretty radical thinking for his time.

To prove his theory, Columbus needed ships and money. He had neither, and no apparent means to get them. So Columbus set out to find another 21 who would help him. He was trying

to accomplish the difficult (find a 21 who will help) in order to achieve the impossible (prove that the world isn't flat). Among the Twenties he encountered were astronomers who could prove him wrong scientifically; experienced seamen who could prove him wrong from their knowledge of the sea; and all sorts of political leaders who could find no merit in such a foolish undertaking. There were economists who demonstrated the fiscal irresponsibility of it all. And there were many others who questioned the mental stability of Mr. Columbus, as well as the validity of his assumption. Columbus had some formidable Twenties opposing his project. But he was a 21 who needed another 21, and he continued his pursuit.

Columbus's quest led him to Queen Isabella, a 21. She too had to overcome her own set of Twenties—the fifteenth-century equivalents of presidential advisers. Each of these advisers had solid reasons why the project should not be started. But the Queen persevered, as Columbus had, and the project was sold, and completed, and everybody lived happily ever after, right?

Not exactly, because, interestingly, Columbus was not completely right. He had sold the project based on the idea that by sailing west he would end up east—in India. From India he could bring many much-sought-after luxuries to be marketed at a tremendous profit. What Columbus didn't realize was that there was a three-thousand-mile-wide continent in the way. Once he reached land, he compounded his mistake by referring to the native population as "Indians" and by attempting to trade beads for things the "Indians" had never seen, much less produced.

These minor mistakes, in the control of a 21, were not enough to spoil the whole project. Imagine what a Twenty would have done. A Twenty would probably never have attempted the voyage in the first place. But assuming he had, the Twenty would have returned and admitted that he was wrong—you couldn't get to India by sailing west. The entire project would have been abandoned, and America would not have been discovered for another few hundred years, when Club Med made it a stop on one of their cruises.

It all turned out all right, of course. This nation was developed and eventually gave the world Big Macs and the banjo. The important thing to remember is that Columbus had an idea, he was a 21, and he sought and found another 21 to MAKE HIS IDEA HAPPEN.

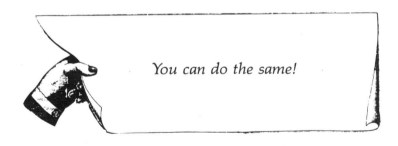

You can do the same!

Now, what about the others who also believed, as Columbus did, that the world was round? We do not have their names recorded in history because they never *accomplished* anything. They had good, valid ideas, but when all was said and done, they had nothing to show. Were these others Twenties or 21s? I believe that they were initially 21s but somewhere on their trek past the Twenties, they accepted the "can't," "shouldn't," or "won't" and allowed the obstacle to become the dead end. This illustrates an important aspect of the Theory of Twenty-One: 21s don't always win. A 21 *can* always win, but the purpose of Twenties is to prevent the success of the 21s, and, occasionally, they win one.

For years after Columbus's exploits, those who had given in to the Twenties regularly slapped their foreheads with the palms of their hands. And they began many conversations with "If only..."

What about the Twenties? Did they lament their misjudgment? Did they witness the accomplishment of a 21 and vow to become 21s themselves? Not on your life! You'll see why later.

There is an interesting difference in the way that Twenties and 21s celebrate their victories. Since the goal of the Twenty is to prevent something from happening, they celebrate by heaving a great sigh of relief. 21s, on the other hand, CELEBRATE BY CELEBRATING. They smile a lot and relish the glory of the moment. Remember that the goal of the Twenty is to accomplish NOTHING, and success for him brings just that—NOTHING.

Now, what about you? Are you among the Twenties or the 21s? Which do you want to be? Understand that YOU CAN BE EITHER! It's a matter of choice.

Do you believe that today, in the twentieth century, it is possible that you could discover a new land or disprove accepted scientific principles? This is an important question, so answer it in your mind before reading any further.

If your answer included the remark "There are no more lands to discover," then you're thinking like a Twenty. And what's even more tragic, you're using the exact same words that your predecessors used five hundred years ago. Stop thinking like that!

Maybe you're not interested in becoming an explorer or revolutionizing science. I know I'm not, at least not right now. But there *are* things you want to accomplish. Once you pass the Twenties and shake off the mind-set of the Twenties, you will realize your goal. Believe it!

This is more than just positive thinking—it is also positive planning and positive action. Thinking is essential as a prerequisite to action, but thinking alone accomplishes little. I'm an avid believer in positive thinking and a fan of the modern father of that philosophy, Norman Vincent Peale. Thought always precedes action. Positive thoughts result in positive action. Negative thoughts never result in positive action. Therefore, positive thinking is essential, but positive thinking does not produce positive results. It takes positive *action* to produce results.

Thinking creates ideas, and ideas are cheap! Sit down by yourself for a few minutes and allow your mind to run in neutral. You may be surprised at how many ideas come into your thoughts. Then try sitting down with a group and brainstorming for the same amount of time. The result will be that even more ideas will come to you. But until something is done with those ideas, they are useless and worthless.

Do Twenties ever have ideas? Yes, and quite often their idea is the same as the idea of a 21. However, the Twenty will think about the idea in terms of why it couldn't, shouldn't, or won't be done and will not take any action until a 21 tries to make a reality out of the idea. The 21 looks at the same idea as an opportunity and evaluates the possibilities of the idea, and then determines how he will pursue it and make it happen.

You will need an action plan. If you've never developed an action plan or if your imagination needs a little jogging, here's an idea to start you off. Take two sheets of paper. Number one sheet from 1 to 20 and set it aside. This is the sheet on which you will list your Twenties who said no, and why they said it.

At the top of the other sheet write the sentences and fill in the blanks, as shown on the sample on the following page.

As you read this book, you will be able to list some of the steps you need to take to accomplish the tasks that will lead to achieving the impossible. As you encounter the Twenties, you will probably identify additional steps that need to be taken.

As an example: suppose you wanted to achieve the impossible goal of having a book published. The tasks that must be accomplished to do that would include writing the book, finding a publisher that handles that type of book, and convincing the editor to review the manuscript. The steps involved might include buying a few hundred sheets of paper, conducting some interviews, and talking to some people in the publishing business. As you approach some of these people, you will learn rather quickly that some of them are Twenties and are determined to stop your book. Don't take it personally. They have probably turned down better works than yours. But don't let their obstacle become your dead end. Just note on your sheet of

I will achieve the impossible goal of _____
_____

In order to do that, I must first accomplish the difficult task(s) of _____
_____

The steps I will take are:

1. *Finish this book.*

2. *Determine to be a 21.*

3. _____

4. _____

5. _____

6. _____

7. _____

8. _____

9. _____

10. _____

paper that another step will be required, and move ahead. Be sure to put that person's name on the list of Twenties so you can keep track of how many rejections you've received. Remember, you must have twenty rejections before you find the 21.

The 21 Worksheet that I prepared for the project of writing this book looks something like this:

I will achieve the impossible goal of having the Theory of 21 book published within eight months.

In order to do that, I must first accomplish the difficult tasks of finishing the manuscript, identifying a publisher, and having my manuscript reviewed by the right editor.

The steps I will take are:

1. *Determine to be a 21 throughout this project.*

2. *Complete the manuscript by [date].*

3. *Identify and contact 21 publishers by [date].*

4. *Adjust my presentation and my plan according to the input I receive from the contacts I make.*

5. _____

6. _____

7. _____

8. _____

9. _____

10. _____

You'll notice several things about my plan that may be of interest to you. First of all, I assigned deadlines for the most important items on the list. Also, I determined to contact 21 publishers when I only need one. The reason for that is my strong conviction of the validity of the Theory of 21. As good as this book is, twenty of the first 21 people I talk to about it will give me a reason why it will not make it into print. But you are reading it, so the Theory holds true. If by some chance more than one publisher likes the book, then I'll be in a better position to negotiate.

Also, note from my list that there is plenty of room for adjustment. There are, at this time, many unidentified steps. As I move through the Twenties, I will see the things that must be done that I cannot see right now. A Twenty stops at the first sign of opposition; a 21 learns from opposition, gets past it, and moves on.

It is important to write down your plans on paper. I don't really understand why, but writing it down solidifies the plan in your subconscious and really helps to make things happen. Having a written guide is also very beneficial in keeping you on track. The first entry on my list of tasks is always to determine to be a 21 throughout the project. I am always surprised when someone who I was sure was a 21 turns out to be a Twenty. When this happens, I occasionally have to go back to my list to remind myself that I am a 21 and that no Twenty, no matter how much I may respect the person, is going to make a Twenty out of me.

Review your lists occasionally. Seeing the progress you are making will encourage you to do more, and the lists will provide direction to channel your renewed energy. When you review your list of the Twenties, try to see if there is a pattern to the type of people listed there. This may give you a clue as to where to look for your 21. Also, keeping the list of Twenties will provide an accurate account of the number of contacts you've made. About the time you're contacting the tenth or twelfth person, it will seem as though you must have gone through at least twenty people. The list will confirm that you are close but not quite there.

There is a difference between strategy and tactics. If you have a background in the military, you may recall that a strategy might be to take an enemy position. The tactics that would be necessary to effect the strategy might include bombing a supply line, performing reconnaissance in the surrounding area, and capturing smaller positions that would be of "strategic" importance. In the corporate world, particularly in marketing, we establish objectives (strategies) and then define a marketing plan (tactics) to achieve those objectives.

It is important to define the exact goal of your project. If you don't know what you're shooting for, how will you know when you hit it?

Then it is equally important to clearly establish the strategy for achieving the goal. If you don't know where you're going, it doesn't matter how you get there.

After you have your sights set on a target, then develop a plan and follow it. You know where you're going, you know how to get there, and now, with a plan, you translate all that "idea-ism" into action. This is where ideas begin to become reality.

In the Theory of 21 there is the goal; there are the difficult tasks, which equate to strategies; and there are the steps, which are the same as tactics. This process is outlined, for each project, by the 21s. The Twenties fly by the seat of their pants—no plans, no strategies, no tactics, and, of course, no goals. Twenties stay in the react mode, while 21s are the ones who act. Find someone who knows where he's going and how he plans to get there, and you're probably talking to a 21. Let me show you how it works.

A friend of mine works for American Telephone and Telegraph. He began his career in the early seventies and, after checking out the turf, established the goal that would drive him in his rise up the corporate ladder. His goal was to be a general manager with A.T.&T. in San Francisco by 1981. He figured out the possible moves that would put him in line for the San Francisco job, and then began to look for opportunities. He wrote his plan down on a piece of paper that stayed with him through several moves. This gentleman deliberately searched out the difficult assignments that no one else wanted, offered to take them on, succeeded at each, and then made sure that the people with clout in the organization heard about his successes. His rise in the corporation surprised even him. He achieved his goal one year ahead of schedule.

What makes this example so significant is that virtually no one thought he could do it. There aren't many general managers in the corporation, and most of them have many years of service. San Francisco is a choice location reserved for the select few, and all of this would require a massive political power base and incredible timing. Essentially, it was impossible.

Make sure you've defined the exact goal you're shooting for.

Whenever anyone would explain the folly of his goal to this man, he would simply put them on his mental list of Twenties. But whenever anyone gave him a boost or showed him a way to move ahead a step or two, he took them with him because he recognized the value and the rarity of these 21s. Not only did he succeed, but all the 21s around him were also given the opportunity to share in the success. That's the way 21s think.

Incidentally, anyone who ever spends any time around this 21 will soon learn his philosophy of life:

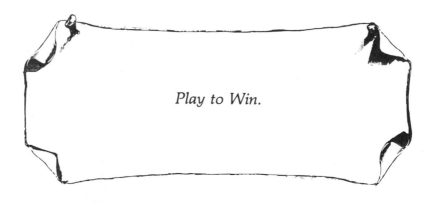

Play to Win.

This 21 lives his philosophy. In everything he does, this man Plays to Win. I have never seen or heard of him accepting any reason for a lost sale or an unsuccessful project. For him, winning is a way of life. (For those working under this gentleman, that can be a source of real frustration.) He even has "Play to Win" written across the back of his yacht.

This man is successful because he understands the principles of the Theory of 21. I've heard him acknowledge that fact in speeches he has made. When he decides that something needs to be done, he finds a 21 or enough 21s to make it happen. His staff is composed of 21s. After setting high goals for himself and for others, he details an action plan and then exceeds his goals. As with most 21s, he delights in hearing the Twenties tell him that what he intends to do cannot be done. There is something about being told that the goal is unattainable that motivates the 21 to achieve it.

The 21 I have just described is typical of the way 21s think. His story is also typical of the successes that 21s attain.

Just because there are no 21s in a given industry or there seems to be no need for them on a specific project, don't be lulled into thinking that there really is no need for them. Some pretty startling things have been accomplished in some seemingly unimpressive places, once a 21 steps in. Usually the first 21 to tackle an area dominated by Twenties comes away with the lion's share of the benefits. So don't be afraid to be the first 21 on your block.

The hamburger industry was already alive and well before McDonald's was born. But because Ray Kroc thought he had a better way to market burgers, tens of BILLIONS of hamburgers have passed under the "Golden Arches" and another 21 is laughing all the way to the bank.

The television industry was controlled by three long-established networks until a country boy from Atlanta launched his cable network. Very few experts gave this venture any kind of a chance. After all, its beginnings were a local, fading UHF station, and even good UHF stations were no threat to the giants. But Ted Turner is a 21, uses 21s, and does not accept negative thinking. His philosophy also exemplifies the thinking of most 21s:

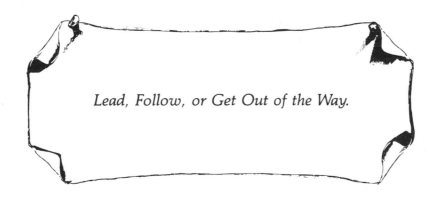

Lead, Follow, or Get Out of the Way.

A couple of young men began building home computers in their garage before the experts thought the market was ready for them. They were entering a market dominated domestically by the giant IBM Corporation and saturated by foreign products from apparently superior, high-technology Japanese companies. "Apple" almost became as synonymous with home computers as "Frigidaire" did with refrigerators. Like most people, I assumed that the most important innovations in computers would be made by IBM or Honeywell. You just never know where or when another 21 will show up.

Nothing can stop a 21, not even another 21. I always enjoy watching two or more 21s going after the same goal. In times like that, the absolute best in human nature emerges. We see the best competing with the best, and what emerges is a performance that exceeds anyone's expectations. When 21s compete with other 21s, they surprise even themselves.

Once, when I was searching for a job, I was offered a position with a company marketing a product that, I was told, "had no competition." That statement was the main reason I declined the offer. How can you motivate people to sell, really sell, if there is no competition? And how do you ever "win" a sale? Where's the challenge?

Most 21s would rather compete with other 21s than with Twenties. Most tennis players and golfers would rather compete with strong contenders than with someone they can easily defeat. There is no fun in easy wins. There is also no growth and little challenge in the simple victories.

Right now, set your goal.

Write your goal down on a piece of paper, as we discussed earlier. Don't wait for a chance to have it typed, and don't worry about the stationery. Find something to write on and with, and put your goal on paper. The back of an envelope or a napkin will do great. Seeing your goal in writing will do something to you and for you.

Decide what the first strategy must be, and write it in the space for "difficult task."

Now list the action steps (tactics) that you will undertake to make this difficult task happen.

As you read this book, you will learn how to recognize 21s, Negative Twenties, and Positive Twenties. You will begin to see who you already know that is going to help you and who isn't. As you identify the 21s, you may find it necessary to change your tactical plan. That's okay.

Even before you have finished reading all of this book you may embark on your quest. That's good: the sooner you get started, the better. When you finish the book (and be sure that you do), make sure that you are in motion, seeking your goal.

Very little happens by itself—you must make it happen. Remember, ideas alone are useless. If you want to build a better mousetrap, start designing a prototype. If you want to become a concert violinist, get the fiddle out and start practicing. If you want to write a symphony, turn off the television, get out some score sheets, and sit down at the piano.

Want to become the vice-president of marketing? Start doing the things that vice-presidents of marketing do. My formula for success in any corporate situation is: STUDY—LEARN—DEMONSTRATE. *Study* what a VP-Marketing is and does. *Learn* what you must know to qualify for the position, and then *demonstrate* that you understand the position by performing like a VP-Marketing. If the position you desire is three promotions away, then map out a strategy for each promotion. Start performing like the next position's best performer. Ask yourself what a high performer in the next rank ahead of you is doing to distinguish himself, and do that. If you cannot do what the star is doing, find out why and fix it.

If your desire is to be the top salesperson in the company, make that your goal. The first strategy for you is to increase your sales. How are you going to do that? What is your plan? If the top salesperson is making an average of five calls a day, make six. If the top salesperson is closing 50 percent of his or her calls, close 60. If you don't believe you can find a way to close a higher percentage, you're a Twenty. Pass this book on to someone who can use it. But before you do, check the final chapter.

No one has as strong a desire for you to succeed as you do. Success requires action. How soon can you start?

I once did one of my famous "guitar talks," where I sing, play, and motivate all in one sitting, for a group in Atlanta. Afterward a man came up to me and said, "I wish I could play a guitar like that." I looked at him and said, "Maybe I can help you. Tell me what happened the last time you tried." He smiled sheepishly and admitted that he'd never tried. Did he really wish he could play the guitar?

Surprisingly, he did. I heard him playing in public less than a year later, and he was pretty good. So watch out, Chet Atkins, there's a 21 loose in your backyard.

Bob Harrington, the "Chaplain of Bourbon Street" in New Orleans, says it this way:

> *Whether you think you can or whether you think you can't, either way you're right.*

The difference between the Twenties and the 21s is that the 21s think they can, and they act on that belief. As a 21 you can expect challenges and conquests, vipers and victories, wars and wins.

A 21 expects the best and achieves it.

A Twenty expects nothing and achieves it.

Make your decision and get started.

No
Optimists
Original thinkers
Overachievers
Allowed!
Violators subject to Ridicule and
the General Ill Will of the
Membership.

STICK NO BILLS

2

THE NEGATIVE TWENTY:
A Human Wall

A former methods engineer at a midwestern chemical corporation tells the sad story of his first career. His function was to devise cost-cutting changes in packaging and handling systems. He would submit his projects to supervisors in two departments: engineering and operations. This man estimates that, 95 percent of the time, he encountered opposition from at least one of the two groups. They would either vote against any of the changes he recommended or tamper with his plan until it closely resembled the original system he was trying to improve. It was a frustrating situation: his job required him to change inefficient methods, and yet he had to fight every step of the way to get those changes accepted. After enduring it for several years, he finally made the break to open the small business he owns and runs today.

A young marketing manager in a major oil corporation had a tough time getting anyone to take his ideas seriously. He could tell that his superiors regarded him as a beginner, still wet behind the ears, who didn't know what was what. The rigid hierarchy, the red tape, the closed ears and closed minds finally prompted this man to take his talents elsewhere. He recently joined a smaller company where, he says, he still encounters resistance to his ideas. Only this time it's positive resistance, meant to refine the idea and not to kill it or steal it.

These two men came up against an attitude that I call "Negative Twentyism," an unthinking resistance to new ways of doing things. It is a characteristic that distinguishes a very large category of people, whom I have labeled the Negative Twenties. The urge to be a Negative Twenty, while quite common, is not a natural response. The methods engineer and the marketing manager dealt with their Negative Twenties the way most 21s do, by getting away from them. But that isn't necessary anymore—the Theory of 21 shows how to work around and through the Negative Twenties. Whatever your job or your goal, you too will encounter Negative Twenties, but you don't always have to let them drive you out—you now have an alternative. You do need to know how to handle them.

In this chapter I will discuss the Negative Twenties, their motives, their attitudes, and their methods. Then I will share techniques that have been successful in managing the Negative Twenties.

The actions of a Negative Twenty spring from a conviction that whatever is being proposed either should not, cannot, or will not be done. A Negative Twenty cannot be budged from this stance. This can work to your advantage if the Negative Twenty's thinking is in your favor. If not, the Negative Twenty will oppose you with all the strength he or she can muster.

For instance, the salesperson who calls on a Negative Twenty who likes the salesperson's product has only to take an order. The Negative Twenty is not likely to order from other vendors, and the account is therefore secure. This is the type of account preferred by Negative Twenty salespersons. It is easy to handle, involves little change, and presents almost no challenge. If, on the other hand, your customer is a Negative Twenty who doesn't know about your product, or prefers another brand, you will have a tough sale on your hands. This is the type of prospect a 21 salesman prefers: one that's challenging and risky.

The person who puts up unthinking resistance to your new idea may be acting out of ignorance, fear, laziness, or a combination of all three.

The ignorant Negative Twenty may lack either the intellectual ability or the imagination to grasp your idea. Perhaps he (or she) doesn't have sufficient specialized knowledge in the area in question. Perhaps he's simply kept his head in the sand, instead of staying abreast of advances in the field. For whatever reason, he lacks the knowledge that would prompt him to give your idea a yes vote. And so his vote is no.

Therefore when you come across someone who greets your idea with the attitude of a Negative Twenty, be aware that he simply may not know any better. If a person does not understand that something is possible, you will probably have little success convincing him that it will be done.

I paid a call on the vice-president of a large insurance service company. He was a Negative Twenty who had attained his executive position as a result of tenure, seniority, and the help of other Twenties who had made it into the top ranks the same way. I wanted to sell him a telemarketing program for his company, a program for selling over the telephone, which many companies, including his competitors, were using. He showed little interest. I knew that his company was losing money, its stock was down, and layoffs were increasing. My recommendation was designed to stop that trend, and I could not understand why he was not receptive to the idea. I completed my presentation and tried for a close; he wouldn't buy. I answered his questions and tried to pry more questions from him, but he still wouldn't buy.

So I asked a few questions of my own. Didn't he know that his competitors were using telemarketing? Weren't his competitors attracting some of his business? In fact, wasn't it this erosion of his business that was causing the problems that his company was having? Wouldn't telemarketing be useful in turning that trend around? He answered yes to all of my questions.

"Then why won't you buy?" I asked.

"Because," he explained, "telemarketing would replace all of our field salespeople, and many of them are my friends."

At some point in his past, this Negative Twenty vice-president had been told that telemarketing would eliminate the need for field salespeople. That was not true. If it had been, I would have mentioned it in my proposal since that would certainly have helped to cost-justify my recommendation. In fact, the telemarketing program would actually generate more leads for the field sales force, and if any change was needed in the number of the sales force, it would be an increase. I overcame his ignorance and eventually closed the sale.

Laziness is the most insidious foe a 21 faces. It may be more apparent in the Twenties. But all of us, even the most driven 21s, are lazy at heart. While 21s fight the tendency; Twenties look for the path of least resistance.

Imagine this scene. You're sitting at your desk. The telephone messages are piled high. You have three meetings scheduled this week, all of which require hours of preparation. Your boss is waiting for a financial report that was due last Thursday. You couldn't put it together because the figures your assistant handed in were incomplete.

You get a call from a new staffer in order fulfillment. He has a revolutionary plan for streamlining packing and shipping procedures. He figures that it would cost X dollars and could be implemented by the end of next year. He's asking for your input. You promise to think about it and call him back. You go back to your own problems. The revolutionary packing and shipping plan? It might work and it might not. It would require months of testing and a big investment. Of course, you look after the budgets, and the guy can't move without your support. But who wants to think about this right now? You don't have the time and you don't have the energy. You know that he's going to call you back for an answer. What's the fastest, easiest way to take care of the matter? Reject the plan. Tell him the time isn't right. You dash off a memo to that effect and put it in the out box. Problem disposed of. Worse luck for him.

Had you been so inclined, you could have given the fellow's plan more consideration. You could have discovered it to be a fine plan, even a brilliant one. But that kind of serious consideration would have required time, thought, maybe even a little research. You didn't want to make the effort. Most people in the same situation would act the same way, you rationalize to yourself. You're right. Most people do.

The most potent motivator for the Negative Twenty is fear. Fear is the strongest motivator for most of us, and Negative Twenties are no different. The two things that a Negative Twenty fears most are change and commitment. There is the fear that change will, somehow, lead to ruin. Life as we know it, with all of its comfortable ruts, ends whenever there is change. Some people cannot handle that: they are the Negative Twenties.

In a business environment, an idea for change means new procedures, new responsibilities, an upset in the routine. Changes aimed at improving efficiency often mean more auto-mation or computerization. People who will be affected by your proposed change perceive that, at the very least, they may have to switch off automatic pilot and think about their jobs again. At worst, their jobs may become less important or un-necessary. No wonder their first reaction is tinged with fear.

A Negative Twenty fears commitment because, all too of-ten, commitment requires offensive (as opposed to defensive) action. Negative Twenties are in the habit of reacting, not act-ing. If you study the old attitudes to which the Negative Twen-ties cling, you will see that they are defensive attitudes. Attitudes like: "Things are going along fine just as they are," and "You can't teach an old dog new tricks." They do not require any assertive or aggressive action but instead are used to defend a lack of action.

Fear of change and fear of commitment can impel Negative Twenties to overcome their laziness and to resist with tremen-dous stamina. Whenever a scared Negative Twenty senses that a change is in the offing, he or she will expend whatever effort is necessary to block the change. The Negative Twenties will spend more energy trying to stop something from happening than it would take to make the new idea happen. It is unlikely that you will ever win a round with a truly frightened Negative Twenty. Most of them can go the distance and hardly work up a sweat.

Maybe you see some of yourself in this discussion of the motives of the Negative Twenties. At least you can begin to understand why they act as they do. Keep in mind that every-one has the potential to be a Twenty and most people have the potential to be a 21. The difference is a matter of attitude.

To kill a new idea, Negative Twenties favor two very pow-erful and lethal responses that can be applied in almost any situation:

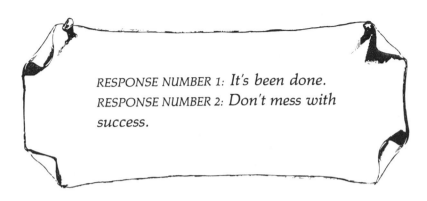

RESPONSE NUMBER 1: It's been done.
RESPONSE NUMBER 2: Don't mess with success.

Other Twenties will accept either response and drop the new idea. They are easily discouraged and accept the first obstacle as the dead end. But 21s will persevere until they ACHIEVE THEIR GOAL, aware that the stock answer is really an obstacle. Negative Twenties use these responses because they are usually successful: Negative Twenties accept them at face value, Positive Twenties allow themselves to be easily discouraged, and many would-be 21s will give in to the persistent application of Responses 1 and 2. Only a true 21 can survive a Negative Twenty who understands the power of "It's been done" or "Don't mess with success."

The premise behind Response Number 1, "It's been done," is that, since it has been done, there is no reason to try it again. If it was tried once before and failed, there is no reason to try it again because it will just fail again. If it was a success, there is no reason to try it again because it would just be a duplicate, me-too endeavor. The astute Negative Twenty can always produce an example from the past that resembles, to some degree, the new idea at hand.

The other line, "Don't mess with success," is used to maintain the status quo. According to too many Negative Twenties, nothing should ever be attempted that might affect the way things are presently being done. After all, the fact that we are doing something today should attest to the validity of the method being used. If it wasn't the right way to do something, we wouldn't be doing it. As long as the Negative Twenty is able to sell this line of thinking, he succeeds in discouraging change.

If the new idea is to begin a new advertising campaign, the Negative Twenties can invoke either response. Response Number 1 can be used to show that previous ad campaigns either produced all the results that were needed or produced little. Either way, a new campaign is not needed. Response Number 2 could be brought in to leave the present ad campaign in place.

If the 21 introduces the idea of writing a motivational book, Response Number 1 is the vehicle for rejection. The Negative Twenty will do a mental data dump and tell the 21 about the large number of books that are submitted to publishers every year and subsequently fail. Well-versed Negative Twenties have good memories for negative statistics. They have total recall when "no" responses are involved and no recollection when "yes" reasons are needed. If the 21 persists with reasons why his or her book can overcome the odds, the Negative Twenty will do a turnabout. The Negative Twenty will then admit that, yes, a number of good motivational books have overcome the odds and made it into print. In fact, so many have been published that now the market is saturated and there is no need for any more motivational books.

In the mid-sixties I met a very old man with one of the most heartbreaking stories about succumbing to the responses of the Twenties. He told me that way back near the end of the last century, when he was at the beginning of his career, an entrepreneur approached him, offering to exchange a partnership in his new business for three thousand dollars. The entrepreneur wanted to produce and market a new nonalcoholic drink that had the ability to refresh and stimulate people after physical exertion. The man asked several people what they thought about the entrepreneur's idea. Some said, "It's been done." There were numerous products of every description already available. Others reminded him that most new products fail. Still others tried to convince the man that he should not mess with success. His money was earning interest in the bank and he already had a good job. The man I was talking to turned down the offer from the entrepreneur. The entrepreneur's name: Asa Candler; his drink: Coca-Cola, "The Pause That Refreshes."

A Negative Twenty might also use a company rule or the latest commandment from upper management to stop you in your tracks. If you're handed this kind of quick no, and you wonder why someone would dismiss an idea without even thinking it through, and then back up his position with blanket rules or instructions that have nothing to do with the specific situation you want to see changed, you may want to consider the following.

When the Negative Twenty heard your idea, he did, just for a moment, entertain the possibility of pursuing it. He put himself into your shoes. But he did not think of what would happen if someone else tried to push it through, he thought of what would happen if *he himself* made the attempt. And being a pessimist and a Negative Twenty, he knew that he would

A special fondness for rules and regulations is the sure sign of a Twenty.

fail, and jumped to the quick conclusion that anyone's attempt would fail. And so by advising you to abandon your idea, he thinks that he's sparing you unnecessary effort and disappointment.

A rule or an instruction from higher up provides him with a safe and easy out. After all, the Negative Twenty didn't make the rule that your innovative plan might violate, and he takes no responsibility for that rule. In discouraging a possible infraction, he's simply following orders. Nobody can fault him for that.

Your best bet is to go to the source of the rule or the instruction. What is the reason behind the rule? What were the circumstances that caused your organization to make it in the first place? Chances are that the company got burned because of an unfortunate course of action, and the policy was laid down to avoid the same mistake and the same results. If you can show that your plan will produce better results, you have a powerful argument to use against Negative Twenties who have a detailed knowledge of the rule book.

Or perhaps the Negative Twenty is simply misinterpreting the instructions that he's received. For instance, when the president of the company said, "We must be careful with all fourth-quarter expenditures," the Negative Twenty department head heard: "Don't spend any money in the fourth quarter." So when you take your idea to this department, one of the middle managers feels perfectly confident in telling you, "The president has said that we can't spend any money on new projects right now."

I have learned through experience to verify such quotes at the horse's mouth. I once presented a business case to my organization, A.T.&T., that showed how it could generate $3 million in revenue over an eighteen-month period with an initial investment of $150,000. This would be accomplished by my company's providing a new service to customer companies that had a toll-free 800 telephone number. This service would identify callers to the toll-free number by region and provide demographic information about them. I erroneously thought that it would be an easy sale. As I moved through the Negative Twenties, I came up against the same response again and again: "The president won't allow us to produce any system that requires nonstandard equipment." Now, can you imagine the president of a multimillion-dollar company refusing a solid business case like this one because of a technicality? The Negative Twenties thought they were secure because nobody would ever contact the *president*. I did, and I sold the project. It generated revenues higher than our expectations, and continues to do so. The persistent 21 will push and ask why his plan can't/shouldn't/won't be done.

If the one-on-one discouragement fails, the Negative Twenty will resort to a public forum: the conference room, the boardroom, or even a social event. The Negative Twenty is not above taking pot shots at the 21 or attempting to humiliate the 21 in front of others. When their backs are up against the wall, the Negative Twenties can be vicious.

An interesting thing happens when the 21 succeeds: the Twenty takes credit for the success that he had originally opposed. This seemingly illogical event occurs when everything goes well. 21s succeed in spite of, not because of, the actions of the Negative Twenties. But once that success is complete, the Negative Twenty steps in to receive some of the accolades. Negative Twenties do this for two reasons: to maintain a feel for what the 21 is doing, and to maintain whatever existing control the Negative Twenty has in the organization. The 21s allow the Negative Twenty to share in the credit partly to help permanently neutralize them and partly out of an optimistic attitude that the Negative Twenty will see the light.

If the 21 is unwilling to share the limelight with the Negative Twenty, the Negative Twenty will continue to work against him. Some Negative Twenties have a strong enough power base to take credit for the success anyway.

I saw an upper-management 21 in a large credit reporting service organization not only refuse to share credit with his Negative Twenties but also to make the tragic mistake of badmouthing them. The 21 resigned after a bitter internal feud.

You should always be aware of where you are in the corporation and where the Negative Twenties are. If you are the CEO, you should understand where the Negative Twenties are, since they are undermining your organization. If you are on your way to the top, learn where the Negative Twenties are who will try to trip you up. If you are anywhere in the organization, take a long look at the front office. Are there Negative Twenties at the top? Look for the telltale signs. Does your company experiment with new policies and procedures, or is business conducted in the same old way from season to season? Does it take advantage of new technologies and the latest in office automation equipment? Is it constantly on the lookout for new markets for its products or services, and new ways to reach those markets, or does it rely on long-established accounts and familiar outlets to keep itself going? Do you have to fill out ten forms to get anything accomplished, and do those forms look as if they haven't been revised in a decade? Time-worn procedures, obsolete equipment and facilities, and lots of red tape are the marks of an organization dominated by Negative Twenties. If this is the case, you may have a difficult time overcoming the blocking tactics of lower-level Negative Twenties.

I took the position of sales manager for an account that was losing badly. The customer did not like our company—its products or its people. I was given the position to try and correct the situation and was told by a great many Twenties that it could not be done. My first move was to interview every member of my organization. The lead salesman was a Negative Twenty and a newly hired salesman was a Negative Twenty. Both of these people had transferred into sales from other departments, both had more seniority with the company than I did, and both were able to offer solid-sounding reasons why things could not/should not/would not be done. They would offer that the customer had rejected similar proposals in the past, that our solution was not in the customer's best interest, or that the customer had decided to go with the competition.

These gentlemen would sit in sales meetings and shoot down every idea for managing the account. They would occasionally offer suggestions (at my insistence), and their new ideas were always reruns of the ways things had been done in the past—yesterday's ideas.

They accomplished little. On occasion, a customer would call in to place an order, to give us some business, only to have one of the Negative Twenties answer the phone and tell the customer, "It's not my job." Fortunately, the customer would have the patience to call me up and chew me out but allow us to retain the sale.

I tried to motivate these two, but found that the account

couldn't wait for improvement, that changes were needed immediately, and so they were sent to other departments. Each of them received an evaluation before leaving and both were disappointed with the marks they received. Since that company was dominated by Twenties, it was not difficult to find another position for each of them; had the company been controlled by 21s these two would never have been there in the first place.

I replaced these gentlemen with 21s, and a year later the revenue from this account had *doubled*, customer rapport was at an all-time high, and the account team was leading all others in results. Sometimes just a few Negative Twenties or a few 21s can make all the difference.

As you try to make any project happen, you will encounter the Negative Twenties. Your first thought may be to try to figure out a way to eliminate them altogether. Giving in to that temptation can be risky. In a sizable organization, the Twenties have the strength of numbers. You never know how much support a Negative Twenty has, and you may be surprised to see who comes forth to rescue him or her. On the other hand, you can't afford to have a Negative Twenty on your side: that's like trying to carry a sack of potatoes in a marathon race. You have a large enough challenge ahead of you without adding unnecessary encumbrances.

The best way to deal with Negative Twenties is to try to neutralize them. Negative Twenties will never support your cause for change, but maybe you will succeed in at least moving them out of the way. For instance, if your impossible goal was to fly across the Atlantic in a hot-air balloon, you would never convince a Negative Twenty to climb into the gondola with you. You might, however, talk him into letting go of the mooring ropes.

There is an art to neutralizing Negative Twenties, and you will become more proficient at managing them with practice. The first step is to determine what motivates a particular Negative Twenty. If you don't know, just ask. Negative Twenties are always eager to tell you why they believe something cannot/should not/will not be done.

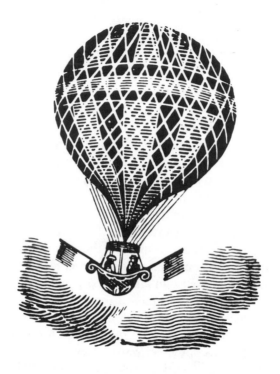

I find that the best way to neutralize the Negative Twenty is to appear to agree with him. Assure him that you understand his point of view, and that you will be the clown on stage making the blunders. Actually, your goal is pure success, but the Negative Twenty will not move aside until you acknowledge, at least to him, that you agree with his assessment of probable failure. At this point, the pride of the Negative Twenty is intact, he has no intention of trying to join you, but he is willing to step aside and give you enough rope to hang yourself.

If you find that a Negative Twenty is motivated by fear, you may have more success than you would in the previous situation. Alleviate that person's fears by showing him that they are unfounded or that the individual will not be affected by your project. Let him know you are willing to take the heat and he may back away and let you have your way. Negative Twenties delight in watching a 21 make a fool out of himself—it solidifies their philosophy.

In cases where the Negative Twenty is motivated by ignorance, take a shot at educating him as I educated the insurance company vice-president about telemarketing. In the section on 21s later in this book you will learn that some Twenties are really 21s who just need a push. I always think it worthwhile to attempt to awaken the 21 inside the Twenty whenever possible. Find out why the Negative Twenty believes he knows that something cannot be done, and try to teach him the truth. Tell the Negative Twenty what you intend to do, how you intend to do it, and what you expect to accomplish. This shows that you have thought through your plan and know where you're going. Negative Twenties never do any planning, so quite often just seeing a plan of action shakes a Negative Twenty into believing that there may be a better way of doing things.

Expect the Negative Twenties. Learn to recognize them, and learn to manage them. You can use your plan to neutralize some of them and maybe even change some of them. The remainder will have to be worked around.

Also, expect the 21s. Read the next chapter on the Positive Twenties, and then we'll discuss a more exciting subject: the 21s.

3

THE
POSITIVE TWENTY:
Doing Nothing Well

THERE is a slippery critter running around your company. I call him the Positive Twenty. He is difficult to identify because he closely resembles a 21, but his accomplishments are the same as those of a Negative Twenty. The Positive Twenty openly encourages you, agrees that there is merit in your idea, even offers to help—and yet never does.

Masters of procrastination, the Positive Twenties can readily give you a solid reason why your idea is good and *should be done*—tomorrow.

Don't spend much time with the Positive Twenties. It is usually wasted. Unfortunately, the only way to know for sure that individuals are Positive Twenties is to allow them to run their course. You will know the Positive Twenties by their faults. Though they talk a good game, when all is said and done, nothing gets done. Since these people are not up front about their intent to block your progress (as the Negative Twenties are), it can take a long time to distinguish a Positive Twenty from a 21.

Even so, there are a few very suspicious signs that may help you sniff out a Positive Twenty. I'm sure there are people in your organization who sometimes make you wonder. You see them from day to day. They are agreeable, seem to fit in well and to command respect. They may appear to be go-getters, look important, and seem busy, and they don't have any huge flops attached to their names. But you can't figure out what it is they actually *do*. You're probably looking at Positive Twenties.

Because Positive Twenties so often resemble 21s, they can rise quite high in the organization. They do not necessarily work or earn their way up, but they are often able to go surprisingly far. To understand how this occurs, take a look at the promotion process in large corporations. Whenever there is a vacancy at any level, people will begin to line up for the job. If the person doing the hiring is a Twenty, then the position is likely to be filled by a Twenty. You understand that Twenties do not enjoy working around 21s and will use their influence to put one of their own in the slot. So do not be surprised if you happen to find one or more on Mahogany Row. When you think about it, it makes sense. Here is a person who never says no but never disturbs the status quo. Such an incredible balancing act deserves all the perks of the executive suite.

The quality that Positive Twenties and 21s seem to share is enthusiasm. The quality that separates the one group from the other is accomplishment. Positive Twenties don't accomplish, not because they aren't as able as 21s, but because they are afraid to try. To try is to risk failure, and Positive Twenties fear failure more than they desire success.

Failure sticks. Twenties will remember the failures even if they forget the successes. Twenties will remind one another that a certain 21 failed at a certain endeavor whenever they need reasons for not doing something.

People in the United States worship winners and loathe failures. We have a low tolerance for the lack of success at anything. Therefore, for many people, it is better not to try

than to try and fail. Positive Twenties always believe themselves to be winners because, by their definition, they never fail.
To them, avoidance of failure equals success.

Positive Twenties are considered to be progressive because
they openly endorse new and innovative ideas. As long as they
are not forced to act on these ideas and run the risk of failure,
then they get along on the reflected credit of other people's
successes.

In the mid-seventies a friend of mine opened a recreational
vehicle dealership. He had already succeeded at a couple of
other ventures and could have retired at the age of forty-five.
But like most entrepreneurs, he had to have something going. A
few months after he began his business, the Arab embargo was
imposed and gasoline prices reached an all-time high. The RV
business plummeted and my friend lost everything.

One day he asked me why so many people thought he was
a failure. He noted that six months earlier these same people
could not say enough nice things about him. Now, it seemed,
he was treated as if he had the plague. Twenties think that
failure is contagious and so avoid those who are afflicted with
it. My friend could not understand how these people could call
him a failure when they had *never even tried*.

The last time I saw him he was on his way to making
another million dollars in the sporting goods market. Such a
failure!

Try to find a company that does not consider itself to be
progressive. In fact, try to find a manager who does not think
of himself as innovative. The Positive Twenties think of themselves this way, after all, and are quick to point out that they
have made changes in the way things are being done.

Several years ago I interviewed the manager of a collection
bureau whose operation was losing money for the fifth consecu-
tive year. I was trying to sell him a system that would automate
his entire collections process, which was manual at the time.
The manual shuffling of paper was astounding. I brought in a
systems analyst to look at the situation, and she threw up her
hands in despair. We calculated that 80 percent of the energies

of the staff of that office were expended on locating pieces of paper. The employees could not be more productive because they could not find the work they needed to do without several hours' search for a single sheet of paper.

My recommendation would eliminate 25 percent of the manager's work force, increase his volume by 30 percent, and improve his bottom line by nearly 48 percent. He indicated that he had already solved the problem by rearranging the desks. He surmised that if the paper flow was reduced in distance (not in function), then each piece of paper would be easier to find.

My approach would eliminate enough labor-intensive functions to eliminate some of the desks. Another of my objectives was to put this company in the black. Moving desks around wasn't going to do it. The point is that this Positive Twenty manager considered himself progressive and his feeble effort to solve the problem perfectly sufficient. He attempted to thwart my efforts without thoroughly evaluating my idea.

Want to know the outcome? We both lost. I went around this branch manager and took my study and my business case to the corporate headquarters. While I managed to convince many of the players, I did not overcome the company's basic philosophy of letting the branch manager have the ultimate responsibility. I lost the sale. A few weeks later, the branch manager was replaced. I wish I had been able to recognize him as a Positive Twenty.

Positive Twenties live in a fascinating world all their own. I call it "life in the middle lane." They stay out of the fast lane, where the 21s are found zipping along. They also avoid the slow lane, which belongs to the Negative Twenties. Life in the middle lane is a series of experiences that involve little more than moving from point A to point B, passing enough people along the way to appear successful. Anyone who passes in the fast lane is considered by the Positive Twenty to be reckless and headed for disaster (failure). The Positive Twenty considers those in the slow lane to be the norm and thinks he is surpassing the average person.

Once you understand the perspective of the Positive Twenties, it becomes easier to understand the rationale behind their behavior. After all, they *are* making progress: nice, safe progress.

Probably the easiest and quickest way to sort out the Negative Twenties, Positive Twenties, and 21s in a crowd is to give each of them an automobile. The Negative Twenty will take the usual route home, sticking to the slow lane. If any obstacles should get in his way, the Negative Twenty will stop until it is cleared. The Negative Twenty will also be oblivious to the fact that everyone else is making better time than he is. He will ignore any available detour because it is untried ground.

The Positive Twenty, as we have discussed, will take the middle lane: faster than his perception of the average, slower than his perception of the reckless.

The 21 will enter the freeway and use *any* lane to REACH HIS GOAL. When speed is necessary, the 21 will not hesitate to use the fast lane. After all, there will not be any Twenties there to obstruct his passage. However, the shrewdest of the 21s know that, to be successful, there are times when the smartest thing to do is to act like a Twenty. The 21 is not afraid to maneuver to move around the obstacles and to achieve his goals.

My wife is one of the most successful 21s I have ever known. She has set and broken sales records everywhere she has ever worked. She has a sports car, and anytime we go anywhere, I drive. She knows how to use every lane (and occasionally the shoulders) to achieve her destination in record time. She holds the record for being able to get through rush hour traffic. She also holds the record in our family for traffic violations and addled passengers. So I drive.

The Positive Twenty has many success stories to relate. This is one reason he seems to closely resemble a 21. These success stories concern those conquests in the middle lane. The Positive Twenty considers passing a poor performer to be a successful achievement, just as he considers avoiding failure to be synonymous with success. To state it simply, the Positive Twenty ignores the successes of those ahead of him and revels in the failures of those behind him.

Another arena where Positive Twenties reveal themselves is

in sports. Every year one team ends up on top—not two teams, one team. Since athletics is so competitive, there is an unusually high percentage of 21s around locker rooms. The winning team is usually the one with the most 21s, but even the losing teams will have their share of them. Teams coached by Twenties or composed of Twenties will end their season close to the bottom of the heap.

The Positive Twenties will end their season as also-rans, but you would never know it to hear them talk. Positive Twenties can tell you about all the points they scored and about how much better they are than the teams that they defeated. Any discussion about the teams to whom they lost is usually short and punctuated with remarks about how the other team played the game recklessly and untraditionally.

Even losing teams will have their stories of victories, but only one team will have the championship. One thing that the Positive Twenties never seem to understand is that it does no good to be the number one quarterback on the last-place team—you still don't go to the Superbowl.

Be careful who you align yourself with—are you signing up with a winner or with the second-best?

Many people ask me: "What's wrong with mediocrity?" Positive Twenties have their share of successes and they aren't suffering from ulcers, overexertion, or stress, right?

Wrong. Positive Twenties spend a lot of energy and wind up with their share of tension as a result of trying to appear to be better than the worst. They also create pressure for themselves whenever they watch a 21 try to achieve the impossible.

The Positive Twenty holds his breath, hoping that the 21 will fail, because success for the Positive Twenty is the failure of a 21. I'll never understand why anyone would go through so much for mediocrity, when only a little more energy would bring stardom. It only costs a little more to go first class, you know.

Positive Twenties loathe the successes of the 21s, and it is this loathing that creates stress for the Positive Twenty. I like to say that the best way for a Positive Twenty to get unstressed is to take his loathes off.

You are probably reading this book because you want to achieve, because you want to be a success. Understand what REAL SUCCESS IS before you go after it.

Positive Twenties are in the magic category between success and failure. They are really neither. Positive Twenties never feel the exhilaration of true success or the agony of failure. And while their apparent successes would lead you to believe that their overall performance was one of achievement, remember that they still are not bringing home the pennant. If you are content with "almost," then you don't need to waste your time reading this book.

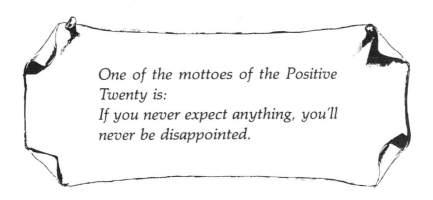

One of the mottoes of the Positive Twenty is:
If you never expect anything, you'll never be disappointed.

Do you remember when the first sub-four-minute mile was run? At one time it was considered a physical impossibility to run a mile in less than four minutes. Some of the best doctors, trainers, and coaches agreed that no human could endure the strain that such an effort would put on the body. Somewhere along the line, an athlete named Roger Bannister did not get the word. In 1954 he ran a mile in three minutes and fifty-nine seconds.

Today, in a major track event, an athlete can run in the mile event, finish in less than four minutes, and not even place among the top three. All over the world there are runners who are training for the mile run. The Positive Twenties are training to break the four-minute mark, not to win the race. They will lose the race and not be disappointed. The 21s are training to WIN THE RACE. They will break the four-minute mark, win the race, and not be disappointed. Following the race, the Positive Twenties will tell about the runners they passed and boast of their speed. The 21s will wear their ribbons and have their names recorded in the record books.

Positive Twenties are the absolute nemesis of salespeople. The Positive Twenty is that proverbial customer who keeps encouraging the salesperson right up to the signing of the contract, and then balks. The Positive Twenty tells you on your first visit that he has already talked to his boss about the need for your product. As you make your initial presentation, he notes that your product is exactly what he needs, just as he told the boss. Of course, there is no need for you to talk to the boss, since he already has the man's ear.

When you think you've done enough selling and the time is right to close the deal, the Positive Twenty will begin to give you reasons why he will not be able to sign today, but may be able to—tomorrow.

I used to wonder why Positive Twenties did this. Some of them just don't like to say no. I guess they think it will hurt the salesperson's feelings. So instead they just string the salesperson along until he or she gives up. Others may assume that the salesperson is just as much a Positive Twenty as they are; that he or she doesn't really expect to actually make the sale and will go away quietly without demanding a decision.

Always remember, the salesperson needs the customer more than the customer needs the salesperson. To sell to a Positive Twenty, you must reverse that.

There's a pattern the Positive Twenties follow when they are about to stall. The first maneuver is to maintain their façade of being the decision maker. Through continued reassurances, they will make it clear that the decision rests with them. They will try to stall until you lose interest so that they can accuse you of giving up. This keeps them from having to make a decision, which they are not likely to do anyway. As you push for decisive action, a Positive Twenty will begin interjecting little comments about having to consult with upper management. He is the decision maker, he reaffirms, but he has to "run the whole thing by headquarters—just a formality." Positive Twenties will request numerous proposals, each one only slightly different from the first. Their reasoning will be that they are trying to make your recommendation palatable to the boys upstairs. They are there to help you. They know what is expected by the brass, and they are only trying to maximize your chance of success. At some point you will tire of this and push for a close. Positive Twenties will either turn you down or—and this happens most frequently—move on to maneuver number two.

The second maneuver is comical because the Positive Twenties take it so seriously. I call it the "Positive Twenty's Martyr Performance." The point of the Positive Twenty's Martyr Performance is to place the blame for a final, delayed "no" on someone else. The Positive Twenty is still positive, but seems to suffer right along with the salesperson, like a martyr. This person was "really on your side," and now you are both defeated, or so the Positive Twenty would have you believe. Actually, he has succeeded in achieving his goal of having nothing done.

This is where the Positive Twenty expects the issue to stop. The 21, of course, is still in hot pursuit of his objective. It is not uncommon, at this point, for the Positive Twenty to turn into a Negative Twenty. He is convinced that the project cannot and/or should not be done and will try to convince you of the same thing. This newly emerged Negative Twenty will be extremely tough to handle, because he already has every detail of your idea and knows any weaknesses. In addition, he may have already mustered support for his position of opposition. Once the Positive Twenty succumbs to the Negative Twenties at the top, it behooves him to align himself with them.

There was a 21 working for a large insurance company as a property design and procurement manager. Her job was to design the office space needed for different areas, locate suitable parcels of property, and negotiate the sale or lease of those properties. Her name was Martha, and her partner in that particular group was a Positive Twenty named Jim. Jim had taught Martha the ropes and thought he had her well indoctrinated.

As time wore on, Martha distinguished herself as a top-notch negotiator and an able designer. Many of her ideas were adopted, but as they veered further and further from the tried-and-true, she met with more and more rejection, both from Jim and from others in the company. Her goal was to change the public's perception of the corporation by improving the appearance of the local offices located all over the country. Martha was also a student of human sciences—the impact that an environment has on an individual's performance. She used that knowledge to improve productivity in the offices she designed.

Martha was well respected throughout the company and was moved up in management. Because of this, Jim, the Positive Twenty, appeared to support her even though he was anything but supportive behind her back. He had two reasons for this charade. One was that if her ideas were accepted, he wanted to be a part of them so that he would know what was going on in his own department and share in the glory. The other was that he wanted to stop anything Martha might accomplish that would threaten the status quo. Over coffee in the headquarters cafeteria, he would openly voice his concern to his buddies about the "little girl" and her strange ideas. But when he was alone with her, he readily endorsed her concepts and offered to speak to his old buddies in the executive suite.

If you have the impression that the Positive Twenty here may have felt that his position was threatened by this young upstart, your impression is probably correct.

This particular corporation was dominated by Twenties and strictly adhered to old-line, conservative business principles. There were few risk-takers, and the management philosophy and operating procedures hadn't changed since the fifties.

Martha, for all of her strong 21 characteristics, was fighting a situation where the ultimate decision makers were Twenties. Jim would tell her that he could sell any decision from their department. In fact, he could sell it only if he wanted to and only if the decision did not radically depart from the norm. Jim was always a Positive Twenty until the brass put pressure on him and turned him into a conforming Negative Twenty. In corporations headed by Twenties, the manager with aspirations knows when it's okay to be a Positive Twenty and when it's smart to be a Negative Twenty.

One day Martha and I were discussing her situation. I already knew most of the details, since I was representing a vendor that wanted to sell the latest in electronic communications equipment to her corporation. My role as salesman for new-location equipment overlapped her responsibility as designer and procurer of new locations. We had both suffered the same frustrations in trying to sell our ideas inside this corporation.

I began explaining my Theory to her, and it was as if a light had come on in her head. "You're right!" she exclaimed. "That's exactly what's been going on."

As we discussed the situation, she developed an action plan for her current project. She began using and circumventing the Twenties. Martha identified a few key 21s who were not afraid to help her. She was able to sell most of her ideas and opened the first truly modern office that the company had ever staffed. In a matter of a few months, over the objections of some of the Twenties, Martha was offered a promotion by one of the 21s.

The reasons she was given for not accepting her ideas varied from the general, such as "We've never done it that way before," to the specific, such as "We just can't afford that right now." The reasons that the 21s gave for offering her a promotion were, "We need some new ideas" and "We need someone who can find the funding." Twenties see obstacles; 21s see opportunities.

A short time later she came by my office to say good-bye. She had declined the promotion. She and her husband had decided to start their own business, a property management and procurement consulting service. Theirs would be a company made up *entirely* of 21s: the two of them. And they are doing quite well.

Martha's story points out a corollary of the Theory of 21: smaller companies have a smaller ratio of Twenties than do larger companies. In fact, for every layer of management there is a proportionate increase in the percentage of Twenties.

This is easily explained by two facts of corporate life: (1) As any company grows, the chief executive officer loses some of his control over the people who staff it. (2) Twenties have to eat, too.

Consider the fact that the top dog in any company loses some control as the business grows. Take any company or corporation, large or small, and examine its origin. You'll find one common thread in the history of most corporations, large or small. Most companies begin small or as a one-person operation. The Bell System, with a million employees, once had a sole proprietor, Alexander Graham Bell. General Motors was formed by the merger of several automobile manufacturers, each having been formed by an individual, such as Ransom Olds, who built the Oldsmobiles. It was Mr. Singer who originally built the sewing machines, and Woolworth's still bears the name of its first proprietor.

When the new company started out, its founder was able to be very selective in hiring new employees. Since most entrepreneurs are 21s, most of the people hired were also 21s. As time went on, the founder began delegating as many of the routine duties as he could, and one of the first to be passed out was the chore of hiring and firing. At some point, a Positive Twenty found his way onto the payroll. Positive Twenties are the pioneers for all the Twenties since they can pass for 21s.

Once the Positive Twenties are established in a company, the erosion has started. The second fact of corporate life now comes into play: Twenties have to eat, too. Twenties are living, breathing human beings and require all the necessities of life that a 21 does. The problem for the Twenties is that they cannot tolerate an environment in which they *must* produce. They need an environment in which they can get by without producing. So once a Positive Twenty has gained entry into an organization, more Twenties follow. The Twenties recruit other Twenties with: "We need more people like you in our company." Their hidden motivation is to produce an environment that is compatible with the Positive Twenty work style. Both Twenties—the one hiring and the one being hired—are served well with this arrangement. One gains the opportunity to earn(?) a living and the other adds a Twenty to help support the other Twenties.

As the company continues to grow, the original 21s and the subsequent 21s rise to the executive offices. Even though the company is being eroded at the bottom by Twenties, the 21s still maintain some level of control.

There comes the day for each entrepreneur when the business is no longer fun. This usually occurs when the Twenties have thoroughly penetrated the organization. At this point the wise 21 will either clean house or sell out.

When we started our own business, my partner and I agreed that we would keep the business small enough to filter out the Twenties before they got a toehold in the company. We also agreed on the conditions under which we would either sell or liquidate the company. The business must be fun, and as long as we enjoy it, we will continue. If it stops being fun we will sell.

Smaller organizations tend to have fewer Twenties because the Twenties are weeded out in the employment process. Larger companies have more than their share of Twenties because there is less control in the hiring process and because once the Twenties have penetrated an organization they tend to multiply.

Here is a graphic representation of this aspect of the Theory of 21. In any organization there is a management pyramid that can be used to identify the management structure. At the top of the pyramid is the top executive. Below the top is a layer of management that reports directly to the top. Each subsequent layer will have more individuals until the final, bottom layer is reached. This layer represents the entry-level employees.

When the entrepreneur 21 begins his business, he surrounds himself with other 21s. His company is staffed at all levels with 21s and is represented like this:

```
            21
      21    21    21
21    21    21    21    21
```

As the company grows and the original 21 begins delegating more responsibility, the infiltration begins. At some point a Positive Twenty (represented as +20 in the chart), because of his resemblance to a 21, makes his way onto the payroll:

<pre>
                21
          21   21   21
    21   21   +20   21   21
</pre>

This Positive Twenty is the pioneer for the Twenties. Once entrenched in an organization, the Positive Twenty will recruit other Twenties, Positive and Negative (−20 on the chart). Then

Where the first Twenty leads, more Twenties are sure to follow.

the Positive Twenty will use his masquerade and/or his longev-
ity with the company to move into middle management. Soon
the management pyramid looks like this:

$$21$$
$$21 \quad +20 \quad 21$$
$$21 \quad +20 \quad 21 \quad -20 \quad 21$$

As time goes by, the organization grows and the Twenties
proliferate. The remaining 21s rise to the top, but because there
are more people in the organization, there are more and more
Twenties. The percentage of Twenties increases until the 21s are
grossly outnumbered. The Twenties permeate the organization
at all levels and finally stop the business from being fun for the
entrepreneur. This is what the organization looks like when the
time comes for the original 21 to bow out:

$$21$$
$$-20 \quad 21 \quad +20 \quad +20 \quad -20$$
$$-20 \quad +20 \quad -20 \quad +20 \quad -20 \quad +20 \quad -20$$

Take a look at the organization in which you work or sell
and analyze the management pyramid. This will give you an
idea of where your proposal needs to be for success. There is no
organization in which an idea cannot be sold. I know that,
because I have sold in all types of pyramids. The organization
in which innovative ideas are most easily sold has this structure:

$$21$$
$$21 \quad 21 \quad 21$$
$$21 \quad 21 \quad 21 \quad 21 \quad 21$$

And the toughest structure in which to sell is:

$$+20$$
$$-20 \quad +20 \quad -20$$
$$-20 \quad +20 \quad -20 \quad +20 \quad -20$$

I won a trip to Acapulco for my sales results one year. The customer organization that I sold to was just like the one above. It *can* be done. It took a lot of time wading past the Twenties and forcing them into a position where they acknowledged they needed me and my product. It was time- and energy-consuming. Frankly, except for the trip to Acapulco and the self-satisfaction, it almost wasn't worth it, because the resources spent on the sales will never be recovered through their profits.

One of the strongest characteristics of the Positive Twenties is their inability to make decisions. Negative Twenties always make a quick decision, and the answer is always no. 21s make decisions readily, maybe not instantly, and their response to good ideas is always positive. But Positive Twenties just don't make any decisions at all. Positive Twenties don't realize that not making a decision *is* making a decision: it is making the decision not to decide.

That may sound like a lot of double talk, but there is an important principle there. Once an issue arises, it must be resolved one way or the other. A decision is made either to act or not to act. If action is selected, the action is either positive or negative. This scenario is carried out *every* time an issue arises. Some people think that they can ignore the issue and it will either go away or else resolve itself. These people are Positive Twenties.

Any circumstance that requires action starts this process. In its simplest form, there is the cafeteria line. The Negative Twenties order "the usual," the 21s order whatever they want, and the Positive Twenties try to find a way not to make a decision. Cafeteria lines demand a lot of decision making. Besides choosing an entree, you must also choose an appetizer, vegetables, a drink, maybe dessert, and so forth. The Positive Twenty will either have the same as the person ahead ordered or choose the daily special where everything is predetermined.

Another common example is the company memorandum. Every day millions of literary masterpieces called company memorandums are created. People categorize themselves by the way they react to these memorandums. The Negative Twenties read the document and begin explaining why any action proposed can't, shouldn't, or won't be done. The 21s will read the memorandum and determine how the information can be used to further their cause. The Positive Twenties won't read it at first, but will put it in a pile of things to do—tomorrow. When the Positive Twenties finally get around to reading it, any action that is required by the memo will not be attempted until absolutely necessary. Positive Twenties do not realize that not doing anything with an action item, such as a memo, is making a decision not to do something.

When a 21 approaches a Twenty with an idea, the Twenty is forced to respond. We have seen that the Negative Twenty will begin his "It can't/shouldn't/won't be done" monologue. The Positive Twenty has to make a decision: to act or not to act. The Positive Twenty will usually choose not to act but to give positive reinforcement that will, it is hoped, detain the 21 long enough for the momentum to die.

This is a common ploy by Positive Twenties because it has been successful. 21s are often deceived by Positive Twenties long enough for the enthusiasm that they have generated to begin to wane. The one thing that a 21 must do is to keep the issue hot. The most important thing for a Positive Twenty is to cool the issue down.

Once a Positive Twenty has managed to slow the project, can anything be done to reverse the damage?

There are a number of approaches that the astute 21 can take when he or she realizes that a Positive Twenty has managed to interfere with the project. The first priority, obviously, is to neutralize the Positive Twenty. Don't fool yourself into thinking that you can convert this Positive Twenty into a 21; remember, born-again 21s are rare. If you attempt to confront and eliminate the entrenched Positive Twenty, you will probably only succeed in creating antagonism and strong opposition. That may be the end result anyway, but you can save yourself a lot of grief by setting your feelings aside, concentrating on your goal, and making an attempt to neutralize the Positive Twenty.

The most important ingredients for neutralizing the Positive Twenty are

---

𝕳onesty and 𝕾incerity

Neutralizing the Positive Twenty usually begins with the expression of gratitude for all the assistance the Positive Twenty has provided. You should be able to do that sincerely because this person has taught you a valuable lesson: a lesson in perseverance or a lesson in Twentyism. Then explain to the Positive Twenty that you want to pursue your idea and that you would like for him (or her) to assist you. You know that in all likelihood he will decline, since participation would require him to risk failure, which Twenties are not willing to do. Nevertheless, your gesture gives the Positive Twenty the feeling that you respect him enough to ask for his assistance. Since respect is usually reciprocated, the Positive Twenty will show respect for you by not openly or actively opposing you. This will keep him from slowing the momentum you generate in the future.

If this process, or some similar effort, does not neutralize the Positive Twenty, move ahead anyway. You have already spent enough of your energy on this person. Understand the Positive Twenty's position so that you can manage the results of his opposition. Put his name on your list of Twenties, make a note of why he said your idea would not fly, and adjust your tactical plan as necessary.

If you are an experienced salesperson, you may recognize this particular Positive Twenty as the "gatekeeper," to use a marketing term for the person who specializes in keeping outsiders out. Selling around the gatekeeper is an art that has puzzled more than a few salespeople. I am about to share with you my tried-and-true method of working around the Positive Twenty gatekeeper.

You should understand by now that your strategy should be

to neutralize the Positive Twenty. You don't want him to work against you, and you don't necessarily want any more of his "help." The secret is to put the Positive Twenty in a position where he can't lose. Convince the Positive Twenty that you will proceed with your plan, and that if it fails, you will be solely responsible. Also convince the Positive Twenty that if you are successful, he will share in the glory.

Sound impossible? It isn't. It isn't easy, by any means—if it were easy, everyone could do it, not just 21s.

The first step is to go back to your 21 Worksheet. Make sure that your goal is clearly in focus. Lay out a plan with strategies and tactics to accomplish your goal. Identify the true decision maker and map out how you will approach him or her. Determine that the credit for every successful move will be shared with the Positive Twenty, whether he deserves it or not. Most Positive Twenties have talked enough about doing positive things that they feel they deserve the credit for anything positive that happens around them.

There is a twofold purpose in allowing the Positive Twenty to share in the success that he (or she) originally opposed. First, if your efforts are successful and you haven't included him, he may quickly turn into a Negative Twenty and begin actively opposing you. Second, no matter how your project turns out, this person will still be the gatekeeper. The next time you confront him he will remember what happened and will respond accordingly.

I was assigned to an account whose gatekeeper, I was told, was a Positive Twenty with a chip on his shoulder. My predecessor had circumvented this person and had succeeded in making a large sale. He also succeeded in alienating the gatekeeper.

In retaliation for our previous success, the gatekeeper rejected virtually every proposal from my company. He started to make buying decisions more rapidly than before, and the decision always went in favor of our competitor. On a number of occasions he did not even allow us to bid on projects.

As soon as I was assigned to the account, I made a list of strategies and tactics I would use to accomplish the impossible goal of selling our product to this company for use in their headquarters location. I knew that once this was accomplished, it would be easier to sell our products and services in other locations throughout the country. The first strategy was to neutralize the gatekeeper, and I made a tactical plan to accomplish that.

The second strategy was to place my proposal in front of the executive vice-president, who I had identified as the true decision maker. I had a list of tactics to accomplish that as well, but concentrated on the first strategy.

Application of the Theory of 21 requires mental exercises. It is very important to think through what you intend to do before you act. This does not call for tremendous intelligence; all it requires is that you take a realistic look at where you are and where you want to be and then decide how *you* can get there. Don't think in terms of how you think others would act; think only in terms of how you, with your unique set of talents and skills, can attain your goal. What works for others may not work for you, and what works for you probably won't work for someone else.

Shortly after I was assigned to the account, I called this gentleman and made an appointment for lunch. This was to be our first meeting, and I knew he would want to unload on me about how miserable our company was. If I allowed him to do that in his office, he would have a major advantage and I would have made neutralizing this person an even more difficult task.

The restaurant I selected served the Positive Twenty's favorite dessert. All through the appetizer and entree he told me, in great detail, how my company had mishandled the account. I allowed him to vent his feelings until I thought he was ready to listen. When the dessert was served, I began to explain my approach to the account. I sincerely apologized for the way he felt he had been treated, and assured him that he would see a new side to our company.

I honored my pledge to work with the Positive Twenty because I believe that honesty and sincerity are the two most important weapons in combating Twenties.

After a week or two had passed, the Positive Twenty asked me to accompany him on a business trip to Washington, D.C. He said he wanted me to assist him in auditing one of his distant offices. I supposed that this was to be a test of my sincerity since I would be expected, by my employer, to make a recommendation to upgrade our equipment in that location. The Positive Twenty would say that he intended to downgrade, that is, to remove much of the equipment there. Then he would watch my reaction.

We made our initial study, and it was obvious that the Washington office sorely needed a new, upgraded system. The Positive Twenty said that he thought a downgrade was the answer. I had reviewed my 21 Worksheet and realized that I had not neutralized this Positive Twenty. I was therefore not yet in a position to contradict him. I bought some time by telling him that I wanted to take my findings back to Atlanta for computer analysis, which was standard procedure.

The last day of our trip, over breakfast, I managed to break some of the ice and have the Positive Twenty talk more about himself. In the course of the conversation, he revealed that he was an avid member of the Optimist Club. He went on to say that he was in charge of the programming for the following month. I explained that I was an after-dinner speaker and offered my services. He was excited to find a fresh voice and a new topic, so we set a date and chose the topic of "Call Me," a motivational talk on communication.

Between the time that we returned from our trip and the time that I addressed the Optimist Club, I polished my proposal for the headquarters location and put together a formal recommendation for the Washington office. The Positive Twenty was not sufficiently neutralized for a major sale, but I did manage to close a few smaller sales that had been lingering around for some time. That reassured me that I was on the right track, and it reassured my boss that I was really out selling. The small sales were nice, but I wanted the BIG ones!

Now, here is how you use *your unique talents and abilities* to move through the Positive Twenties. My talent is public speaking and I used it to the fullest the day I spoke to the Optimist Club. I gave it everything I had.

There was a standing ovation following my talk—a rare occurrence, I learned later. The Positive Twenty became the hero of the hour and was warmly congratulated by the entire membership for finding such a fine speaker.

The next day I was in the office of the Positive Twenty with my headquarters proposal. The time was right. I explained that he and I could go before his superiors and sell this idea. I expected him to decline, and he did. I explained that he could be the hero on this one—all I wanted was the sale. He had declined, but he moved out of the way. His reason: "they" would never buy it.

I sold the headquarters project and, as a result of that and other successes, was promoted before closing the Washington deal. My successor on the account was Ed, one of my favorite 21s. Ed was aware of what I had accomplished and knew a lot about how I had managed to succeed with this Positive Twenty. Ed and I talked and mapped out a strategy for him to follow to close the Washington proposal.

Ed acknowledged that he was not a public speaker and would have to use his own talents to be successful on this account. We assessed Ed's abilities and decided which of his strengths would work best for him in this situation. He then defined his strategies and tactics and attacked the account.

Ed's strongest talent is his ability to get along with almost anyone and his uncanny ability to accomplish the seemingly impossible tasks inside his company—tasks such as finding out-of-stock equipment, cutting shipping and installation times, and gaining "impossible" concessions for his customers.

I introduced Ed to the Positive Twenty gatekeeper, and immediately Ed asked if there was anything he could do for the customer. Just as we had anticipated, the customer asked for a favor. He wanted an obsolete, unavailable device for one of his distant offices. He had asked for this device before but had been turned down by the Negative Twenties in our company. Ed showed his sincerity by procuring the item and having it delivered to the office where it was needed.

From then on, whenever anyone in the customer's organization needed anything from our company, they would simply tell the Positive Twenty, who would pass the request on to Ed. Ed was making the Positive Twenty a hero inside his own organization, just as I had done, but he was doing it his own way, with his own skills.

After a few successes, Ed figured he was ready to ask the Positive Twenty for the order on the Washington project, the deal I hadn't been able to close. After a few false starts involving the expected, menial rewrites of the proposal, Ed became convinced that the Positive Twenty was stalling, waiting for the momentum to dissipate. Ed pushed for the close and received the expected reply: "they" wouldn't approve it. Ed explained that he would again make him a hero, but the Positive Twenty wouldn't accept his promise—too much risk. However, he did move aside, neutralized by Ed's hard work, and Ed sold the Washington project.

Ed's story points out how he used his talents to successfully move around the Positive Twenty. Maybe you don't think that the ability to work with people or having the determination to work hard are talents. And maybe you don't think you have any special talents. Think again. Most people enjoy the things they do well, and the things you do well are your talents. Therefore:

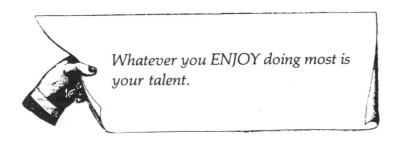

Whatever you ENJOY doing most is your talent.

Because you enjoy it, you don't think of it as a skill, *but it is.*
Applying the Theory of 21 allows you to use your talents

and skills to move around and through the Positive Twenties to accomplish your impossible goals.

The Positive Twenties are everywhere. They are the public officials who don't deliver on their promises. They are the service people who promise repairs that are not made or are not made in the agreed-upon time. The Positive Twenties are the members of your church or civic organization who accepted positions of leadership supposedly to make things happen but have accomplished nothing. Positive Twenties are the people in your organization who have begun numerous projects and completed few. The person who attends committee meetings week after week, promising that the report will be ready next week, is a Positive Twenty. "Next week" is another way of saying "tomorrow." Positive Twenties have enough initiative to begin a project, but not enough to see it through.

To salespeople, the most aggravating of them all is the Positive Twenty gatekeeper. For everyone, the most exasperating is the repairman who never completes his task. No matter how long he keeps your item or how often he attempts to correct the problem, it never works right. I have used the Theory of 21 to master these Positive Twenties, too. I rarely have trouble with service people any longer.

Several years ago I bought a new car. Like many new automobiles, it had a few problems that needed correcting. I left it with the dealer for a day and picked it up, only to find that the trouble was still there. I took the car back and had a heart-to-heart talk with the rookie mechanic who had been assigned to my car. He vowed to fix it but, being a Positive Twenty, said more than he did, and the car was no better off. Since sincerity is an essential element in managing the Positive Twenties, how could I honestly manage this one? What could I *sincerely* say to him to neutralize him?

When I came to pick up my car and found that it still wasn't repaired, I sought out the young mechanic. I told him how impressed I was with anyone who could begin to understand the complex inner workings of that car and explained that I thought there was a manufacturing defect in the car since he could not fix it. He knew that wasn't so, and so did I. But it got him off the hook and out of my way. As I approached the service manager to explain about the "manufacturing defect," the mechanic began looking more closely at my car. Suddenly he found the source of the problem, fixed it, and saved the service manager a lot of grief from me. My praise for his work convinced the mechanic that he was a hero.

From then on, whenever my car was taken in for service, the same mechanic always took care of it personally. Instead of doing the least he could do, he usually went the extra mile. When the bumper needed work, he repaired it and also tightened the fan belt and adjusted some other things—all at no charge. Was the Positive Twenty mechanic evolving into a 21?

On rare occasions, Positive Twenties do evolve into 21s. The metamorphosis changes one human being from a difficult obstacle into a potent innovator. Success and failure are reserved for the 21s, so when a Positive Twenty assumes the responsibility of trying to become a 21, at that moment he *is* a 21.

You are about to learn more about the 21s and about how to mold a 21 out of a Positive Twenty.

The most exciting part of the Theory of 21 is the 21s. We have spent enough time on the Twenties; now for the best part. . . .

4

THE 21

AN old man was sitting at the gate to the city when a stranger approached.

"Tell me, old man," said the stranger, "have you lived here long?"

"All my life," was the reply.

"Well, tell me this: how will I find the people here?" asked the stranger.

The old man thought for a moment and asked, "How were they where you came from?"

"Terrible," the stranger responded. "They were the biggest bunch of thieves and cutthroats I've ever seen. They would steal the shirt right off your back."

"You'll find them the same way here," the old man said.

Some time later, another stranger approached the city, saw the old man, and asked the same question: "How will I find the people here?"

The old man thought for a moment and asked, "How were they where you came from?"

"Oh," said the stranger, "they were the finest bunch of people you would ever want to meet. They'd give you the shirt off their back."

"You'll find them the same way here," said the old man.

It is true that we find what we are looking for. 21s find success, and they find it everywhere they go. As you will discover in this chapter, there are reasons why the 21 finds success in the same areas where the Twenty finds failure. Twenties and 21s all live in the same world, meet the same people, and see the same events. The 21s come away from these experiences with accomplishments while the Twenties come away with nothing new.

Two men, Mr. A and Mr. B, enter a restaurant and both order lobster. The waitress brings a platter with two lobsters on it. One lobster is large and juicy, the other small and dried-up. Mr. A reaches over and takes the nicer lobster, puts it on his plate, and begins breaking off the claws. Mr. B says, "Well, I guess that's the rudest thing I've ever seen." Mr. A replies, "Why? What would you have done?" Mr. B says, "I'd have taken the smaller one." "You've got it!" Mr. A responds.

To understand the Theory of 21, you must first understand the difference between "natural" and "average." There is also a difference between "normal" and "natural." The average American is 8.5 pounds overweight. That is not natural. The average American smokes 5 cigarettes a day—average but not natural. Sneezing and coughing are natural; filling one's lungs with a carcinogenic tar isn't. The normal person will also do things that are not natural. Too many "normal" people believe that things that have not been done cannot, should not, or will not be done. There is nothing natural about that. Change, and the occurrence of new events, are natural.

If you study the behavior of children, you will see that children believe that almost anything is possible. Adults call it "make-believe" when a child pretends to be a doctor or a scientist. But in fact, for that moment in time, the child *is* a doctor. If left alone, I believe that the child would eventually become a doctor. Of course it would take an extensive education and so forth, but until a child is told that he is not a doctor, he will continue to believe that he can be one.

The child is "told" that he is not a doctor in a variety of ways. If his brother or sister becomes ill, the parents either nurse that sibling back to health without any assistance from the child, or they call for the help of an actual doctor. Either way, the child gets the message that he is not doing the doctoring. Even if he offers to help, the parents are likely to shoo him away.

But take the case of Jimmy. At the age of four, Jimmy announced that he wanted to become an aeronautical engineer. His parents didn't understand why or how he knew he wanted to be an aeronautical engineer, but they never attempted to discourage him. By the time Jimmy finished third grade, he also knew that he wanted to work for Lockheed. After achieving honors at Georgia Tech, Jimmy spent a year flying a helicopter in Vietnam and distinguished himself in that role. There were numerous job offers for Jimmy because of his education and experience, some of them quite lucrative. Jimmy turned them all down and waited for an offer from Lockheed. He is still at Lockheed today.

YOU AND EVERYONE ELSE WERE BORN 21s. Twenties are the products of our society, a society that endorses and encourages the unnatural attitude to oppose change regardless of its potential to improve our lives.

Somewhere in our past, we were taught the attitudes of the Twenties and that mind-set was reaffirmed by most of the people we knew, including our friends, our schoolteachers, and our ministers. This is normal and should not be surprising, since most people are Twenties and teach what they believe. We lose the innocence of our youth, become Twenties, and then become the makers and molders of more Twenties. We begin to expect to find Twentyism everywhere we go, and we are usually not disappointed. This is the average, normal scheme of things. But it is not natural.

You can usually tell what a person expected from any given situation by what they found. I have seen people leaving a motivational seminar with a bounce in their step and determination in their eyes, while others, the Twenties, left grumbling about the "phony hype." The first expected motivation and the others expected phony hype.

Twenties do not expect new ideas to sell, and their ideas don't sell. 21s expect their ideas to sell, and they do. People who expect to be passed over for promotion usually are. Others think that they do not have a chance of winning a contest or a game, and they lose. 21s believe that they will win even when all others may be telling them that they do not have a chance, and they emerge winners.

I have seen this phenomenon occur in the greatest and smallest events of life. During the busiest shopping season, people tell me that they have to park a great distance from the malls and shops, and they do. I always park by the door. Some people expect illness and look sick; others expect health and look well. Two employees join the company at the same time, one expecting success and one mediocrity. The first retires from the top floor, the other retires from a lower floor.

As you may have surmised, this is all to point out a basic fact:

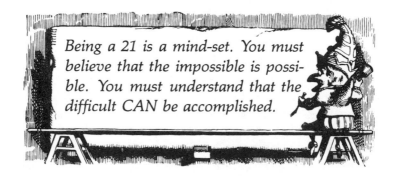

Being a 21 is a mind-set. You must believe that the impossible is possible. You must understand that the difficult CAN be accomplished.

So what distinguishes the Theory of 21 from any other teaching that espouses the virtues of having the right attitude?

None of this is new to those of you who are students of positive thinking. Numerous books have been written and thousands of seminars have been conducted to teach the power of positive thought. But the problem with some positive thinkers is that they are unable to translate their positive ideas into results. The positive attitude is there, but the accomplishments are missing. This is where the Theory of 21 can be of invaluable assistance.

Remember, the basic difference between Twenties and 21s is *accomplishment*. There are many people running around with positive attitudes, who want to succeed, but who have not begun to accomplish their goals. If you are one of these people, this chapter is for you.

For the Theory to work, you must first have a positive attitude. It is unlikely that you would even attempt to become a 21 in the first place without a strong, positive attitude. I mention it here to remind you of the importance of having the correct mind-set.

But positive thinking alone is not enough. There must be action if anything is to be accomplished. Generally speaking, greater action produces greater results. To maximize the results, maximize the actions. To maximize the actions, have a plan. It is really that simple:

Positive Thinking + Positive Action = Positive Results.

The more you add to the left side of the equation, the more you add to the right side.

The Theory of 21 incorporates a proven method to maximize the results, the successes, the accomplishments you will achieve. For the 21 who knows how to use other 21s and knows how to move around the Twenties, nothing is impossible.

NOTHING IS IMPOSSIBLE. You can accomplish your goal, whatever it is, by applying the principles of the Theory.

The first step in being a 21 is to

Have a goal.

The second step is to have a plan, but without a goal there can be no plan. Know what you want!

In my seminars and in one-on-one situations, I ask this question: "What do you want to accomplish with your life?" To me, that is the most important issue. I do not understand why anyone would choose to live one day at a time with no thought for tomorrow and no goals. Fortunately, I see very few people who give no thought to goals at all. What I do see is a lot of people who do not exactly know what they want, or who know what they want but aren't sure how to go about attaining it. Is that where you are?

Right now, not two minutes from now but right now, think of what you would do with the rest of your life if you could do *anything*. I want you to "blue sky" on this one for a moment. Then I want you to formulate a one-sentence answer. We will expound on it later.

Formulate your answer. Repeat your answer several times in your mind so that it will be implanted there. Each word is critical.

Now let's discuss your initial response to one of the most important questions that you will ever address. Did your response begin with something like: "Someday I would like to . . ."? If it did, we have identified the first obstacle to your attaining your impossible goal. Pull out every calendar you can find and see which one has a "someday" on it. It doesn't exist and it will never come. Waiting on "someday" is the single biggest obstacle to becoming a 21. It has tripped up more potential 21s than any other single obstacle, and has become a dead end for quite a few Twenties.

Imagine what you would do with the rest of your life if you could do anything at all.

There is a normal tendency to act when the time is "right." I am convinced that the "right" time comes along so infrequently that it is not worth the pursuit for anyone. If you are waiting for the "right" time, the "someday," then plan to stay right where you are from now on.

Wally Amos decided to bake cookies for a living. He knew that was what he wanted to do, and he was convinced that he would enjoy doing it and that he would succeed. His Twenties explained why he couldn't, shouldn't, wouldn't succeed at this business. The major bakeries had the market sewn up. Wally was undercapitalized; he did not have the credentials to run the business or to raise the money he needed. And besides, the price of sugar was at an all-time high—the time was not right to start a cookie business.

One of Wally Amos's other goals was to live in Hawaii. After Famous Amos cookies took off, Wally opened another plant in Hawaii and moved there. His cookies are now sold nationwide, are considered a delicacy by some, and command a premium price. When Wally travels to the mainland, he brings along his favorite toy, a custom vehicle. Wally Amos does everything with class, and there is no "wrong" time for a class act. Incidentally, thirty minutes with Amos will make a 21 out of almost any Positive Twenty.

If Wally Amos had waited for the price of sugar to drop, the cost of labor would probably have gone up, and many other components of his overhead, such as rent, flour, and packaging costs, might have increased in cost. So the time would not have been "right" then, either. But more important than that, while Wally was waiting for the "right" time he would not be selling cookies. He would not be building a business and he would not be making money from his cookies. What he would have been doing is working at something that was not what he really wanted instead of something he really enjoyed.

A portion of Wally's market went away every day he delayed. Every day people ate cookies and the cookies they ate weren't Wally's. The same is true for you. Every day that you delay making the commitment to begin your dream is a day *lost* to your dream. If your goal is to publish a book, then every day that you delay writing the book is a day that one of your potential readers buys another book. If your goal is to publish a magazine, then every month that you delay is an issue that will never be published. If your goal is to be the vice-president of your department, then every year you procrastinate and avoid making the decision to map out and follow a plan is one less year that you will be a VP.

So, the next step:

Set a date.

Set a realistic date but don't put it too far off. You will learn that once you have a targeted goal, things may begin happening faster than you may have thought possible. People more often set their targeted date too far off than too soon, so be realistic but plan on stretching yourself.

I asked Diane what she would do if she could do anything she wanted. Diane is a reporter for a business newspaper, and her goal is to have her own magazine, one along the lines of *The New Yorker.* I asked her to formulate her goal, and she began with the dreaded "someday." I made a suggestion: "Do you have any friends in the paste-up department at your paper? Ask one of them to make a mock-up of your first magazine cover. You decide the typeset and the cover story. Then take the cover home and hang it in a prominent place where you will see it every day." Once Diane does this, she will begin adding the headlines for the cover and this will cause her to think of the people she will need to write the stories behind the headlines. Events will occur and have a significant impact on her: she will begin thinking of them in terms of potential articles for her magazine. These events should assist her in establishing a target date for the first issue. She will meet people who will strike her as potential employees, partners, or backers for her magazine. Once the date is established, her magazine will start to become a reality.

You need a point of focus, some visualization of your goal. If your goal is a new position in your company, write up a newspaper announcement or an internal memo of your promotion, and date it. Have a goal. If your goal is a job with another company, make yourself a new business card with the title you want on it, and date it. Have a goal.

If your goal is to increase the membership of your organization from 25 to 250, then find a picture of 250 people and write the name of your organization on it and the date that you *expect* the group to attain that membership goal. Then hang the picture in a place that will often remind you of your goal and your targeted date.

What was your goal? Formulate it in your mind again. Does it sound something like: "Someday I want to..." or "Someday I wish to..."? If so, we may have identified the second obstacle to your achieving your impossible goal. Even if you replace the "someday" with a specific date, you still have a weakness. The Theory of 21 does not work for wants or wishes. As long as your goal is a want or a wish, it assumes little credence in your mind. We all have pipe dreams and daydreams, and for the most part they never happen. To have a goal that will survive the Twenties, you must *know* that your goal will happen. If you are not convinced, you will have little success convincing anyone else.

Compare the goals above to this one: "Within the next six months I will have completed the manuscript of a full-length novel." Or to this one: "By this date next year I will have the title of Regional Sales Manager." Do you see the difference? Can you feel the difference?

BY RESTATING YOUR GOAL AND PUTTING IT INTO POSITIVE, CONCRETE TERMS, YOU WILL CONVINCE YOURSELF AND OTHERS THAT YOUR GOAL IS GOING TO HAPPEN! What you sense on the outside is not as important as what is going on in your mind. We are learning that not only is the mind programmable, but it takes its programming from our deepest beliefs. If you recite something long enough, your inner self will begin believing it and your mind will program it to happen.

When you were a child, did you ever hear the story of *The Little Engine Who Could*? In this story, a small steam engine has to pull a long train up a hill—a seemingly impossible task. However, because she believes she can, and reinforces her belief by chanting "I think I can," she succeeds.

In earlier chapters we discussed the Twenties and noted that they were easily discouraged by other Twenties. When a Twenty has an idea, he does not usually take the time to convince himself that the idea *will* happen. His mind is not convinced. So when he hits the first obstacle, he is easily put off. In many cases, if you could get to the Twenty at that point and tell him that his idea was a good one, he would try again. But then the next obstacle would become a dead end. He will not be able to persevere because he is not really convinced.

Convince yourself.

You know that you have the talent and the ability to accomplish your goal, don't you? You know that you understand what it takes to achieve what you want to achieve, and you know that you want it. So all you have to do is *do it*. If you are having doubts about your own abilities—we all do from time to time—try this: think about individuals who are already doing what you want to do and compare yourself to them *objectively*. Are they superhuman? Is their intelligence at the genius level? I doubt it.

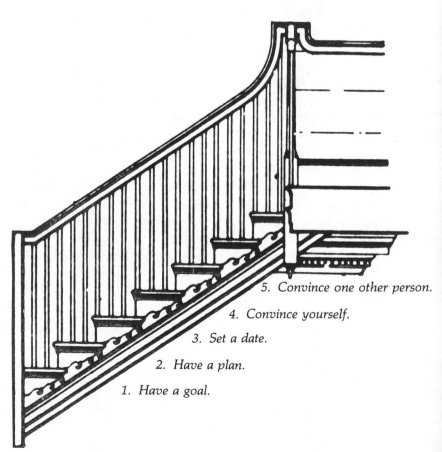

5. *Convince one other person.*

4. *Convince yourself.*

3. *Set a date.*

2. *Have a plan.*

1. *Have a goal.*

The only difference between you and the people who are doing what you would like to do is just that: they are doing it. And the main reason that you aren't doing it is because you haven't tried.

Convince yourself, and the next step is to

*Convince one
other person.*

You are not ready yet to take on the Twenties, so as soon as you are convinced that you can accomplish your goal, go convince just one other person. If you are married, I recommend that the one person that you convince be your spouse. If you're not married, choose a friend who knows you well. You need to select a person who knows you well so that you cannot fool them in case you're really not convinced. The whole purpose of this effort is to solidify your conviction of your ability to accomplish your goal and to create synergy between you and someone else.

At this point you wil have created momentum. As I said before, without commitment, this momentum can be stopped with the first obstacle. What you need now is a plan, a track to follow that will direct the momentum.

Make a 21 Worksheet.

At the top of the page write:

---

*"I will accomplish the impossible goal of _____.
In order to do that, I must first accomplish the difficult
tactic of _____. The tasks I will use to do that
are: _____.*

(List your steps.)

The Theory of 21 forces you to identify and examine the
steps you need to take to accomplish your goal. Break them
down into their simplest tasks. Don't leave anything out, because no matter how trivial a task may seem, it still must be
done. These tasks are the benchmarks that will show you and
others the progress you are making toward your goal. Most
benchmarks should also be assigned a target date. As you identify each step, set a target date to complete that step, and then
do it. These interim deadlines will motivate you one step at a
time, and the composite of them will give you a more accurate
feel for the date that your goal will be accomplished.

Up until now, you may never have begun the effort to be

what you want to be. And for that reason, you have come no closer to attaining your goal. What you should be able to do now is take the first step.

If your goal is to achieve a higher position in your company—say, two levels above your current position—then the first strategy you need to detail is how to rise to the next level. What are the tasks that are necessary to accomplish that? Do you have any idea where to start? I have seen case after case where an idea never became reality because the person with the idea did not know where to start. This is a common malady that has tripped up a lot of people. There is an easy way to begin.

Instead of looking at the entire problem or opportunity at once, try breaking it down into smaller components. Two privates in the Army were assigned to a disciplinary work detail and told to move a two-ton pile of rocks. One looked at the pile and said that it couldn't be done, it was too heavy. The other looked at the pile and saw only small rocks, none of which were too heavy. Trying to decide on a plan of attack for achieving a new position in the corporation may not be as easy as moving a pile of rocks. If you simply cannot identify the first step, then the first step is obvious: identify the first step. You do that by asking people who should know, "How do I begin?"

This may be your first experience with a Twenty, so on the back of your 21 Worksheet make a place to list the Twenties and their reasons for telling you that your goal cannot be accomplished. It should look something like this:

NAME	REASON
1. _____	_____
2. _____	_____
3. _____	_____

Whom are you going to ask? You are looking for advice on how to begin your quest toward your impossible goal, so what type of person are you to approach? First of all, find someone who has done what you want to do and someone who tried to accomplish your goal and failed. Both can give you enormous amounts of information. Using what you know already about 21s, try to find 21s, not Twenties.

Ask these selected people how to start, and write down what they say. If they tell you that you cannot/should not/will not accomplish your goal, ask them why and put their name and reason on the back of your 21 Worksheet. If they say something like: "It won't be easy, but . . ." you have identified a valuable resource; take in all that they will tell you. They are being honest: if it were easy, everybody would be doing it. However, do not equate difficulty with unpleasantness. Even though your trip to your impossible goal may be difficult, it will also be enjoyable.

I have found that the person who says "Success came easily for me" either had a head start with some family money or else enjoyed the work so much that he or she never saw the difficulties. Neither case will offer much help to you in trying to start off on the first step.

In 1979 an immigrant named Joseph Nakash was competing with blue-blooded Gloria Vanderbilt for the designer jean dollars. Fifteen years earlier, Nakash was sleeping in bus and train stations because his $40-a-week job as a stock boy would not provide him any better. Mr. Nakash was able to save enough money to bring his brothers to this country, and the three of them forged the Jordache fashion line. They each had to work long hours, but their hours and working conditions were an improvement on their previous life-styles. Their experience and common sense told them that the way to succeed was to advertise like crazy, and so they poured money into the now familiar Jordache ads. Gloria Vanderbilt and the Nakash brothers began the race from different starting points, but reached the finish line together. They faced some similar hurdles and encountered their own unique hurdles. But all of these people enjoyed the race toward their goal.

Why would people who are successful want to talk to you? They probably do not have the time to spend talking to everyone who asks for their time. How are you to gain an audience with them? As a rule, they are very busy people. If they are ahead of you in the corporate structure, the rules may say that you cannot talk to them. If they are public figures, there will be rules that govern their time and their interfaces with other people.

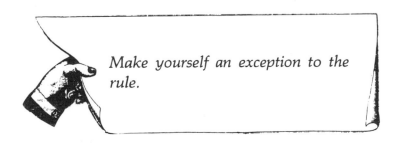

Make yourself an exception to the rule.

This is the heart of the Theory of 21. This is also the most often misunderstood aspect of the Theory, so I will take some time to explain it now. You are to make yourself an exception to the rule, but *you are never to break the rule*. There is an important difference. First of all, understand what rules are.

Rules are not laws, and there should be no exceptions to laws. For example, it is a law, not a rule, that requires us to stop at red lights. Trying to be an exception to that law could only be catastrophic. But rules are different. Rules are made to control the masses, and the masses are, you guessed it, Twenties. Twenties want and need rules because rules are the first step in blocking change. Rules are an easy out, and rules can be a valuable tool for controlling the Twenties. But if you look closely at most rules, you will see that they have control and limitation as their purpose. There are exceptions to this statement, of course, such as rules that require a certain amount of effort in order to be obeyed. Sales goals are rules that cause something to happen. But like most action-stimulating rules, sales objectives are governed by more rules.

For instance: the rule is that all salespersons must sell one million dollars' worth of goods every year or they will not be paid a bonus and will be subject to dismissal. That's the action-provoking rule. Behind this is a list of rules about where the salespersons can sell, what they must sell, what paper work must accompany each order, and so on. These are limiting rules.

If you break a rule, you are subjecting yourself to the possibility of all kinds of misery. But to be an exception to the rule means that you have permission from someone in authority to circumvent it. Why would anyone want to do that for you?

When I go into a place that has a sign that says "No Personal Checks Accepted," I write a check and the proprietor takes it. Why? Because he thinks my check is good and because he wants the business. And that in a nutshell is how you can be an exception to the rule.

There are two elements:

> You must appear worthy of the exception.
> There must be something in it for the person responsible for enforcing the rule.

The first element is something you earn. If you want to be a third-level manager and you are currently a first-level, the rules say that you must serve some time as a second-level. That is a rule for Twenties. Suppose a person clearly demonstrates that he can perform at the third level and that he is the best person for the job, that he is worthy of it. Then the rules will be bent to accommodate the change.

Take the case of Carol. She is a junior-level clerk. She is performing the tasks of an absent first-level manager and is doing quite well. Her responsibilities include a few secretarial tasks, many first-level managerial tasks, and an occasional second-level task. Someone inside the corporation realizes that this junior-level clerk is doing a first-level manager's job and alerts the department head. Carol has not yet become a 21 and does not know that she can be an exception to the rule. Her organization has one 21 in it. What do you think will happen if the rule states that only senior-level clerks can be promoted to management and Carol is one level lower?

This is an actual case. The 21 in the organization said that since Carol had distinguished herself in the job, she should be moved into management, even if the paper work had to be floated in such a way as to first make her a senior-level clerk and then promote her again. The Twenties said that only a clerk with more seniority could be promoted into the job, even if the person chosen lacked the skills to perform the task. The department head tried for the easy way out by saying that he would turn the tasks over to an existing manager.

The absurdity of all of this is that the criterion being used for making the decision is not the quality of the person's work but her level, a nebulous term and possibly the result of hiring and promotional errors. If a clerk is doing a manager's job, doesn't he or she deserve a manager's title?

As this book goes to press, this problem is still not solved. It has lingered for months. The clerk is still doing the managerial task and the Twenties are still unhappy. The only thing that has changed is that Carol has attended a coaching session on being a 21 and is in the process of making herself an exception to the rule.

You need to identify the rules that are keeping you from your goal and then to identify the person who can grant you permission to sidestep the rule. The Twenties listed on the back of your 21 Worksheet may help you pinpoint the rules that are causing you problems. As your list of Twenties grows, review it to see if there is a specific issue that keeps cropping up and needs to be addressed. If you must have specialized training to achieve your goal, then enroll in a class. If the opportunity you desire is in another state, then notify management that you are mobile and willing to relocate. As long as the reason, the rule, is valid, obey it. But if the rule is just for Twenties, find a way to become the exception to the rule.

Earlier in this book I told you about the time I had a solid business case for a new telephone service—proposing that for a $150,000 investment my company could generate $3 million over eighteen months. I was handed the same line over and over again. It could not/should not/would not be done because the president of the company had said that there would be no more special systems using nonstandard equipment. That was the rule. The rule was valid because manufacturing such equipment usually consumed a lot of resources, while special systems rarely returned much revenue. So because most special systems were not worth the effort, all special systems were to be refused. My business case showed that we were worthy of the exception to that rule and also showed that there was a tremendous payoff for the person who had set down the rule. I made myself an exception to the rule, and the special system was developed.

You must be worthy of the exception and there must be something in it for the person who has the power to bend the rule. In Carol's case the benefit to the department head is that he will have a recruited manager who is proficient in her work.

In business situations, the most powerful motivation for a manager is more business. For those of us in sales, this is a daily fact of life. The purchasing agent may not let us in to see the executive who would ultimately use our product because the executive has a rule that all salespersons go through the purchasing agent. This keeps the executive free from all those salespersons who are Twenties. I always talk to the executive. How?

The purchasing agent has the ability to screen vendors from making appointments with the executive, but I have yet to meet a purchasing agent who has the authority to screen the exec's mail. As soon as the executive realizes that he is reading a sales pitch, however, he forwards the letter to the agent. So I write a letter that discusses the business problem and a solution that will bring more business to the executive. I never mention product until the very end, and usually by then the person reading the letter is convinced enough to want to see and hear more— this time in person. He sees the value to him: more business.

What you need from now on is a network of people who can help you define the steps necessary to achieve your goals. There must be value for them if you are to gain some of their time. And you must appear worthy.

Appearing worthy is a matter of image. What kind of image are you projecting? If you were an executive, would you be comfortable around a person like you? If your goal is to be a doctor, would a doctor see you as worthy of his time? Image is more than appearance or dress. It is also what you say and how you say it. It is an attitude that permeates the way you think, the way you walk, and the way you sit. As you make yourself the exception to the rule, make sure you appear to be an exception to the rule.

In our seminars on preparing college graduates for their entry into the marketplace, we stress the importance of their image and the impact that it will have on their future employer's first impression of them. It amazes me that many upper managers lose the sense of importance of image and try to regain it when they need to be an exception to the rule. Image management is an art that should be practiced throughout your career.

Can you recall a time when you made yourself an exception to the rule? Can you recall an instance when someone else did? How about the times you have gone to a restaurant that does not accept reservations and have been told that there are no available tables, only to have someone come in behind you and be seated? How about the person who can always find tickets to the sold-out concerts?

In business, you repeatedly see the managers who seem to be the exception to the rule. The salesperson who constantly exceeds his or her quota is not subject to the rule that says all employees will be at their desks promptly at 9 A.M. That rule is for the Twenties who have to be managed as they try to not produce. Get the idea?

Now, back to the issue of why an executive or a public figure or any individuals who believe they are important would grant you any of their time. First of all, *are* you worthy of their time? Of course you are, but how do you tell them? Is there anything in it for them? There had better be, or you won't get to them.

Second, remember that their time is valuable and you must be judicious in taking any of it. Make your request for time as succinct as possible. This will tell the person that you can be brief and still convey information. Practice this request over and over until you are comfortable with it. You will have the ability to demonstrate that you are worthy of this person's attention—you have a need and you will not waste his time.

If you are a CEO or other senior officer in a company and you are approached for advice by someone who appears worthy (and sincere), how are you likely to react? Will your response be that of a Twenty: can't/shouldn't/won't be done, violation of the rules of protocol, and so on? Or will you respond as a 21: I will see you for fifteen minutes on the third; I cannot fit you into my schedule now, but if you will call Mr. Jones . . . ?

Gaining the advice you need to start out on your goal will probably be the first opportunity for you to use the Theory of 21. From then on, the process is the same: identify the person who has the information you need or who has to perform a task for you, and approach that person as someone worthy of their time and with a payoff for them.

Now rewrite your goal. Include the date that your goal will be realized and affirm that it WILL happen.

Here is a question that many people I interview cannot answer: In one sentence, can you define "success"?

You want to be a success, right? You know people who are successes, right? But do you really know what success is? If you don't, how will you know when you have attained it?

Success for you and success for anyone else are two different things. You will attain your success and you will live with it. So what is success? Some people tell me that success is a Mercedes, a big house, or lots of money, but those are products of success. If your goal is success and success for you is a lot of money, there are plenty of ways to attain your goal and most of them will leave you feeling less than successful even when your bank account is bulging.

Now compare your definition of success with your goal. Are they compatible? If not, then change the one that is out of place. Now LET'S GO BE 21S!

Put together your 21 Worksheet(s), look at your target dates and strategies and tactics, and start out on your quest. NOW.

One final note about 21s. I am often asked if I believe that nice guys finish last, and if that's so, aren't all 21s "bad guys," since they finish up front? The answer is that it is true that nice guys finish last. It is also true that nice guys finish first. Being a nice guy does not determine where you wind up in the race, it only determines how you run the race. Being a 21 should have little impact on others' perceptions of whether or not you are a nice guy. Twenties may think that you are becoming snobbish because you are not spending (wasting) as much time with them as you used to, and there is a normal resentment that some people feel toward others who are successful. Be aware that some people may not appreciate 21s, but don't let that deter you from setting your goal to be one.

Believe it or not, almost everyone loves a winner. Be a 21 and be a winner. And be a "nice guy" about it all.

Want to make someone else into a 21? Wouldn't it be great if everyone you dealt with was a 21? Read on. . . .

5

MAKING A 21

OD never created a Twenty. He made only 21s. Twenties are the products of mankind, but have the ability to convert back to 21s.

There is within each of us a child—an innocent, malleable mind that entertains the impossible. It is this mind-set that permits 21s to be 21s. When this kind of thinking is buried under negative, pessimistic attitudes, the end result is Twentyitis. To make a 21 out of someone afflicted with Twentyitis, you must first push the negative thoughts aside to allow positive thoughts to enter.

If you watch children at play, you will see how they allow their imaginations to dominate their thoughts and their activities. Their uninhibited minds give them the attitude that almost anything is possible. At play, a child can be a doctor, police officer, schoolteacher, parent, or astronaut. This thought process bridges over into reality when children assert that they intend to be doctors, police officers or whatever when they grow up. They *believe* their goal is possible, and at that point they are 21s.

Thomas Edison was discouraged by his schoolteacher from entering any profession requiring him to use his mind. The teacher even sent a note to Edison's mother declaring him to be untrainable. Herschel Walker was told by a high school football coach that he was too small to play the game.

These are people who overcame the negative influences and continued to be 21s. But how many other young minds succumbed to the discouragement of the Twenties? We might have had the electric light and the phonograph sooner if some of Edison's upperclassmen had been stimulated instead of stymied.

The motivation for the actions of the Twenties is often honorable. They are convinced that they are doing the right thing, based in part on their own experience as Twenties. The unfortunate part is that they are actually acting out of ignorance—ignorance of a person's real ability and ignorance of the Theory of 21. For all their effort, they could just as well have stimulated their charge into maximum performance. Since you have read this book this far, you know that the potential for success resides within *everyone*. There is no excuse for you to discourage anyone. But don't confuse the lack of discouragement with encouragement. If you are to make a 21, you must encourage the person actively, not just refrain from holding him or her back.

Why would you want to encourage a 21? What's in it for you? Those are the types of question a Twenty asks, not the types of inquiries I expect from a 21. A 21 knows why he or she wants to make another 21: to improve the individual, to improve the company or other organization, even to improve the world. Everyone benefits from the successes of a 21, even the Twenties who opposed the 21 initially. For instance, we all enjoy the benefits of Thomas Edison's work, and even those who told Herschel Walker that he'd never make it as a football player enjoy watching him play football.

But the conversion process for reclaiming 21s can consume

a great deal of time and energy. And since not every Twenty is capable of change, the time and effort may yield no improved results. There are ways to improve your chances of success in converting a Twenty, and there are ways to increase the likelihood of success.

First of all, understand who can and who cannot be made into a 21. It takes a lot of practice to be able to recognize the salvageable from the unsalvageable, but there are some signals to look for before taking on a Twenty as a project. The Twentyism or Twentyitis must not be too ingrained, and the Twenty *must desire to be a 21.*

If the Twentyism or Twentyitis outweighs the desire to become a 21, or if there is no desire to become a 21, there is little hope of converting the Twenty to a 21.

Terminal Twentyitis! Is there no cure for his affliction?

Tom came into sales as a Positive Twenty and wanted to remain so. The only problem was that he was assigned to work for me. Positive Twenties can survive in sales, and occasionally, under the right circumstances, so can a Negative Twenty. But I had no room for either in my organization, so I attempted to convert Tom. The first step would be to make him *want* to be a 21, and the second step would be to convert him.

Tom saw the others in the group, all 21s, and saw the accomplishments that each had achieved. He also saw the honors and accolades that his peers were receiving. He wanted to be a 21, or so he told me.

I would give Tom projects, easy ones at first. As long as I was actively involved, pushing and pulling, he responded like a 21. However, as soon as I handed over the reins to him, Tom reverted to being a Twenty.

Tom brought me a problem (which, of course, was really an opportunity) and presented five reasons why a certain project could not be completed. We started with the first one and mapped out a strategy and the tactics to accomplish the strategy. This first problem was a lack of equipment for the project. I asked Tom where some equipment might be found and what could be done to have it shipped to the customer's location in Miami by the due date. Once the synergy started, Tom became excited and began developing the tactics to overcome this obstacle.

By five o'clock that afternoon, after a few false starts and several trips into my office for reinforcement and encouragement, Tom announced that the equipment had been located and one more telephone call would ensure delivery of the equipment on time. Tom would make that call the next day.

"Why not now?" I asked.

"It's quitting time," he replied.

Apparently the look on my face prompted Tom to make the call. But as he moved through the other four obstacles, similar symptoms of Twentyitis kept emerging. At one point the project was dropped for lack of a certain piece of paper. Another time the dead end was a person who would not return Tom's telephone calls. I thought that my motivation and Tom's mounting successes would cause him to become a 21. I was wrong.

The due date was missed because at the last minute an old engineering friend of Tom's found an obstacle, and Tom accepted it. Despite his recent successes, Tom's desire to be a 21 was not strong enough to overcome his chronic Twentyitis.

And despite all of my efforts, Tom remained a Positive Twenty and eventually had to be transferred to another department. His problem was one of continued exposure to Twenty managers. Even after Tom saw and appreciated and even admired the accomplishments of the 21s in our group, the years of negatives would still take over and cause Tom to think and to respond as a Twenty.

There are the Twenties who *can* be converted, and they come in all different colors, sizes, and shapes. They come from both sexes, all ages, and every vocation. The only things that they have in common are that they are not terminally afflicted with Twentyitis and that they desire to be 21s. And you can help to instill the desire to become a 21.

There is great value in converting a Twenty to a 21. There is value to the born-again 21's employer or other organizations he belongs to: the new 21 accomplishes more for the organization. There is value to the born-again 21's family: the new 21 becomes a better spouse, parent, or sibling. And there is value to you for having converted the person: you have another 21 to help you accomplish your goals. But your having improved another person should be enough incentive for you to want to make more 21s.

Just as Twenties tend to propagate themselves, so do 21s. When you make a 21 you are starting an entire line of 21s.

Remember that 21s are not people who lack the qualities of a Twenty but people who possess the qualities of a 21. There is an important distinction. As you achieve success in removing the negative thought process from a Twenty, be sure that you replace it with the positive thought process. Simply eliminating the wrong type of thinking will possibly neutralize the Twenty

for a while. But if left unattended and without positive reinforcement, the person will revert right back to being a Twenty.

Making a 21 is a swap: the Twenty GIVES UP THE NEGA-
TIVE and TAKES IN THE POSITIVE. It is a two-step process.

We live in an age of change. For this reason, we need 21s
more than ever before. Can you name any field that is not
undergoing rapid change? My doctor tells me that he can no
longer keep up with reading the bulk of what is being written
about his area of specialization, much less the entire medical
field. My attorney pointed to a box of volumes and said that
they contained the changes in the state law for this year. I can
no longer do my own income taxes because of all of the changes
in the tax laws. My mechanic must now know almost as much
about my car as the person who designed it, and more than a
design engineer knew just a few years ago.

In the old businesses and in the new professions, change is
encountered daily. Students entering specialized data-processing
schools are being told that before they can finish their education
some of what they learn will be obsolete.

There is no escaping the impact of change. Twenties believe
that they can stall the change long enough for it to go away.
They are mistaken. Twenties believe that things are still done
better the old way, and again they are wrong. The time is
approaching when being a 21 will be essential for survival. The
opportunity to do things the old way, to block the inevitable
change, and to assert that something cannot/should not/will
not be done is becoming rare.

Twenties will not die a natural death. They will oppose new
ideas down to their last breath. You will need the ability to
convert Twenties to 21s for as long as you live. There will
always be Twenties who will want to hold back progress. When
they do accept change, they will do so reluctantly, slowly, a
little bit at a time.

Determine who should be a 21 and decide that you will help
mold him or her into a winner. If the person already wants to be
a 21, the first step is accomplished. If, however, the person does

not want to be a 21 or does recognize the need to be one, your first step is to try to instill in him or her the desire to be a 21. There are several ways to do this.

ONE

Be an example for the Twenty to look to. I have found that almost everyone wants to *be* a success but few are willing to *become* a success. When they can see that an ordinary person is making it, they can begin to visualize themselves becoming successful, too. But they need guidance—they need a plan.

You can be an example in little things and in bigger things. Don't ever pass up an opportunity to be a 21 in front of a Twenty. When you are with a Twenty who you think has potential, look for opportunities to demonstrate the Theory of 21. Point out other 21s to the Twenty and use them as examples. The Twenty needs to understand that being a 21 is a way of life.

TWO

Then tell the Twenty that he can be a 21. Some people don't know they can succeed because no one ever told them that they could. I know that sounds awfully simple, but I wish you could see the eyes of people who have never been told of their own potential until I tell them. It's usually the brightest part of my day! Most people have been told more times than they can remember that certain things cannot/should not/will not be done. They have accepted that as a fact, and for them it has become a dead end.

THREE

Still another method of convincing the Twenties that they have the potential to be 21s is by demonstration. Show them something that you are accomplishing at the moment. Show them your 21 Worksheet or your strategic plan. Demonstrate to them that you know what you are going to accomplish and that you know how you intend to accomplish it. When my friend who became a general manager for A.T.&T. in San Francisco in his predetermined time frame showed his plan to people, they became convinced that he would achieve his goal. When he showed it to his subordinates, and showed how he was on track with his plan, it demonstrated to them that they, too, could achieve their goals, and they would begin following my friend's lead.

You need to demonstrate that being a successful 21 is not luck and is not a fluke. It is the result of planning and execution. If there is little or no apparent reason why you are succeeding, then the Twenty is justified in thinking that your success is just luck. But when a Twenty sees that you are attaining your goals through a systematic plan, it demonstrates to him that it is possible for him to attain his own goals.

FOUR

The fourth method is the most convincing: participation. Make a Twenty a part of your plan, and the chances are he or she will emerge a 21. This participation can be as minor or as heavy as the Twenty will allow. It can range from observation to total involvement. You can involve him in the planning or the execution stage. Involving the Twenty also gives you the chance to use all of the other methods of proving to the Twenty that he can succeed; i.e., you can now encourage him, inspire him through example, demonstrate your plan.

I was a young technician with the telephone company and had been given the opportunity to demonstrate a new testing computer to some middle managers from around the country. Less than an hour before the presentation/demonstration, one of the managers involved with this show came into the room and asked me to provide writing tablets, pencils, and other supplies for the attendees. I had tried earlier to do that but had been blocked at the supply room by the supply clerk. There had been a rash of people taking such supplies out (school was starting), and no one could have more than one pad or pencil. None of my explaining had any effect, so I came away empty-handed.

I tried to explain all of this to the manager. Since he was a

21, it sounded like nothing but obstacle noise to him. He handed me a telephone and told me to call the supply room and have them box up what we needed. I did, and got the response you might imagine. Then he told me to call the operations manager and explain the problem. I did, nervously, and was told that he would check on it and call me back. The manager went on about his business as if the problem had been resolved. The phone never rang, but five minutes later the supply clerk walked in with our supplies. I learned about being a 21 through participation.

Another kind of participation that can produce fast results is what I call the "deep end" method. One of my best friends and I wanted to learn to swim, so our fathers took us to the city pool. My father taught me the techniques of kicking, arm strokes, breathing, and the rest, and had me practice them over and over. My friend's father threw him in the deep end and let him learn, rather quickly, how to get out. The "deep end" method can be used when you need a quick conversion.

Have you ever been in a crisis situation? Crises bring out the 21 in each of us, even if we've been accustomed to going along as Twenties. We find that we are able to accomplish the

impossible and that we are able to do it expeditiously because we have to. It amazes me that we prove that we can accomplish the seemingly impossible tasks when crisis strikes, but then revert to being Twenties as soon as the crisis passes. Why is that? Why will people stretch themselves beyond their limits to return something to the way it was, but will resist expending the same amount of effort to improve something? We see pictures on the nightly news of hundreds of people filling sandbags to stop rising floodwaters, working for days with little or no rest. Then we see city parks fallen into near-ruin because the municipalities do not have the money to pay someone to do the repair work and the citizens don't care enough to volunteer.

The Theory of 21 explains this phenomenon by showing that most people are Twenties and that Twenties will expend whatever energy is necessary to have things remain as they have always been.

Another method, then, to encourage a Twenty to become a 21 is to create an artificial crisis situation for him. Put him in a position where he must *do* something. Then, as long as he has to be doing something anyway, show him how to accomplish, not restore.

An artificial crisis is any situation where a person feels that something dreadful will happen if he or she does not respond. Examples of artificial crises are sales objectives and sales quotas that appear to exceed the salesperson's ability to sell. Another artificial crisis is the deadline. The importance of any deadline can be exaggerated to the point that it becomes an artificial crisis.

I took over the account team and found that there had not been a true salesperson on the team for some time. There were two types of position: account executive (sales) and market administrator (sales service). The account executive was a Twenty, and after some effort I realized that I would not be able to convert him within a reasonable time, so I made my plan to replace him. The market administrators were all 21s and were right where they should have been, except for one. I determined that he should be the new account executive. He was selling, he was sharp, and his talents were being wasted on his current assignment.

I approached this person and asked him to accept the new position. He declined and gave as his reason the fact that account executives were on commission and his paycheck would depend on his ability to sell. Being an account executive would be a crisis situation for him, since his wife didn't work and he had two small children at home depending on that paycheck. I asked him to think about it anyway.

Later, he said he had talked it over with his wife and he would stay in the lower position of sales service. I asked if I could talk to his wife.

As a sales service person he knew he was a 21. But as a salesman he saw himself as a Twenty.

In January this 21 became an account executive and his home, his house, his car, his boat were all riding on his sales. He was in a league with nearly a thousand other account executives and had a sales quota that was a challenge, to say the least. Many of the other account executives had years of experience in the job, but few of them considered themselves to be in a crisis situation. Experience had shown them they would survive. This account executive was not sure that he would survive, so, for him, this artificial crisis was quite real. As I said, that was in January. In September he received a letter from the vice-president congratulating him for being the number one account executive in the country. I was prouder of the letter than he was.

A classic example of managing Twenties and 21s occurred recently with the divestiture of the Bell System.

The Bell System was a hundred years old, had led the world in technology through its facilities at Bell Laboratories, and was providing the highest-quality communications service in the world. Independent surveys had determined that the company was one of the best-managed in the world, even though it was the largest, with a million employees.

There was nothing wrong with the company, but the communications industry was changing. For the first time, Bell was facing competition. However, the competition was penetrating only in the highest-profit areas, leaving Bell to try to compete while still providing service to the lower-profit users. In 1969 the Carterfone decision opened the door. Numerous lawsuits followed in the seventies, and it became apparent to the brass at Bell that change was inevitable.

There were the nay-sayers in the communications industry who said that Bell would never be able to compete because of all of the "dead wood" inside the organization. Since Bell was the largest organization in the world, it followed that it would have the most Twenties. Since many of Bell's efforts were almost totally regulated by local, state, or federal tariffs, the Twenty mentality was functionally okay at the task level.

Following the Carterfone decision, Bell began mapping out a plan that would change the communications industry forever. For the plan to succeed, there would have to be 21s at all levels. Since Bell had never really had to compete, the first area of concentration was marketing. The executives at A.T.&T. developed and executed a plan to attract the finest marketeers from IBM to the Bell System.

The sales force was analyzed, and a plan was developed to identify the 21s, build 21s out of the Twenties who could be converted, and make it easy for those who could not/should not/would not be in a competitive sales position to move into other jobs. A dynamic sales force was emerging from what had been considered the lackluster sales group of Bell.

The new marketing guru used several tactics to achieve the strategy of building 21s out of the existing sales force by placing them in crisis situations. Since the existing sales force was divided geographically, he changed the lines of division to the customer's industry. Industry specialization became the order of the day. The salespeople were given the incentive to strive for the ultimate level of proficiency: industry consultant. For many of the old-time salespeople, this was a crisis situation. The game had changed entirely—all of the rules had changed. Those who could not change with the times simply left sales.

It was not essential, as some think, for the success of Bell that industry specialization be adopted. It was only essential that enough change be interjected to start the sales force thinking in a positive direction. If the existing organization had already been industry-specialized then the change to geographic dispersion would have been equally as successful, as long as it created an artificial crisis. The point is, there was a plan, the plan was being followed, and members of the sales force were being encouraged to become 21s.

Then the new marketeer introduced "compensation," as the Bell System termed commission sales. Those who could sell and who sold would be paid more than those who couldn't or didn't. This weeded out more of the Twenties. Those who could adapt to change but who could not commit to risking part of their salary to their ability to perform also left sales. They saw compensation as a crisis.

Then the product line was scrutinized to determine which products were the most profitable and would continue to be the most profitable in a competitive environment.

All this time, the litigation and regulation continued. Less-informed people thought that Bell was missing the mark on some of the products and services. Some saw Bell as "sluggish." In fact, there was a plan, Twenties were being molded into 21s, and the plan was being executed. The litigation and the regulation could have created a real crisis had Bell not been planning around it.

The litigation was mounting. The Justice Department's lawsuit was into its sixth year and second judge. Congress was trying to enact a new Communications Act, since this high-technology industry was still operating under the Act of 1935. More suits and litigants emerged almost daily. The water was coming to a boil, but would Bell be ready?

I was walking past the television department in a department store, and there on the screen were the chairman of the board of A.T.&T. and a representative from the Justice Department announcing that a settlement had been reached in their lawsuit. Bell would divest itself of itself; the plan would be detailed within six months and would be in the implementation process in less than a year. They were actually going to pull it off!

What amazed me the most about all of this was that the executives at A.T.&T. actually *thought* they could do it. Imagine the mind-set that entertained the thought that the largest corporation in the world—with a million employees, over $60 billion in revenue, and billions in assets—could actually be divested to the satisfaction of the Justice Department, Congress, and even competitors.

Most of us assumed that the original deadlines would be extended for a year or two, but we were wrong. Part of the plan included moving expeditiously as soon as an agreement was reached. This would again make 21s out of people who had not been severely challenged in some time. In less than a year a new company had to be born.

As the plans for the new company developed, some of the employees at Bell were given the opportunity to choose to stay with the regulated side of the business or move to the deregulated company. This was the ultimate weeding out of the Twenties, since Twenties saw a move to the new company as a potential crisis for them. Only 21s chose to move into the uncertain world of American Bell. Some 21s chose to stay with regulated Bell, for a number of different reasons that do not need to be discussed here. The point is that the new company, American Bell, was beginning with a large share of 21s in its ranks.

The original dates were met. In order to accomplish this, every phase of the beginning of the new company had to be expedited. This artificial crisis was the impetus that forced virtually everyone involved with the transition to act as a 21.

After American Bell was in place, the sales quotas were announced, and as you might expect, they were significantly higher than many people had anticipated. It occurred to me when I learned about these quotas that the marketing guru was still at it, still building what will be one of the strongest sales forces in this country.

I can tell you that few things in your life will be as rewarding as building a 21. When you see the difference in a person who has learned that he or she can accomplish the impossible, when you see how it affects every aspect of this person's life, you will understand that the effort was well worth while.

You will also have another 21 to help you achieve your impossible goal.

Who is the Twenty that you would like to convert into a 21? Is it someone who works for you or reports to you? Is it someone who is important to you? Or is it you? Identify the person, determine to convert them into a 21, and then develop a plan. Sound familiar?

"I will accomplish the impossible goal of *converting [NAME] to a 21 by [DATE]*. In order to do that ..."

6

CONCLUSION

PERHAPS you have the impression after reading this far that 21s are some kind of superhuman—the legendary leaders and achievers who can only be found at the very top of the heap. Perhaps you think that this kind of superstardom is beyond your reach. The 21s I've named in the book—Steve Wozniak and Steve Jobs of Apple Computers, Ted Turner, Wally Amos—are certainly headline-makers, but I've chosen to use them as examples because most readers will recognize their names. The truth is that being a 21 is not a matter of brilliance, charisma, or limitless ambition. The virtues that set 21s apart are much more humble: confidence in oneself and in one's ideas, a can-do attitude, a willingness to persevere despite repeated discouragement, the patience to search for those rare individuals who will buy your ideas, support them, and help to make them a reality.

Maintaining your confidence in yourself and your ideas is perhaps the most difficult requirement. After all, untested ideas and untried plans are easy to abandon, especially when the majority of the people you ask will give you convincing reasons why they won't work. We're used to soliciting the opinions of other people—our colleagues, our seniors, our friends—and we usually listen to what they say. And when the idea being discussed has truly never been tried, we're in a vulnerable position to begin with: we don't yet have the proof that the idea will work. My advice is: go ahead and *listen* to other people's reactions to your projects. Absorb whatever information they give you. But if you get a negative response, don't let your confidence be shaken. It's not your fault, and it's probably not the fault of your idea. You could very well be talking to a Twenty. Don't let Twentyism and negative thinking get you off course.

Ask yourself this question first: have you ever been hit by a great idea, only to drop it because you weren't convinced you could make it work? Have you ever seen someone else take the same idea and turn it into a resounding success? You can be sure that that person, whoever he or she was, faced the same doubts, the same uncertainty, and the same resistance you did. But that person somehow overcame his doubts and was able to maintain the level of confidence needed to sell and complete the project. You can do the same.

If you're able to keep your confidence up, then the ability to persevere in the face of nay-sayers, do-nothings, and other human obstacles will follow. You'll patiently listen to the objections of the Twenties. You'll patiently adjust your plan and your strategies as you go. You'll carefully and diplomatically work around the Twenties until you find a 21 who will lend his support. And, if you persist, you'll one day see your ideas become real.

What will happen then? Having succeeded in reaching one goal, your confidence will become even stronger, and it will become even harder for any Twenty to stand in your way. Once you've proven to yourself that perseverance pays off, that same persistence will become a habit. You'll be secure in the knowledge that you are a 21 and that if you search, you can reach like-minded 21s who will help to speed your success. You'll be convinced that the time and effort it takes to be a 21 and to find other 21s is always worthwhile. Whatever your quest, you'll be virtually unbeatable.